A Culinary History of

MARTHA'S VINEYARD

A Culinary History of

MARTHA'S VINEYARD

Thomas Dresser & Joyce Dresser

Foreword by Marnely Murray

AMERICAN PALATE

Published by American Palate
A Division of The History Press
Charleston, SC
www.historypress.com

Front cover, top, left to right: Lobster bake at the Katama General Store. *Courtesy of Marnely Murray*. Pumpkins on display at Middletown Nursery. *Courtesy of Joyce Dresser*. Fresh oysters on an oyster tour with Cottage City Oysters. *Courtesy of Marnely Murray*.
Bottom: Trap fishermen spreading a net, waiting for fish to swim into it. *Courtesy of Martha's Vineyard Museum*.
Back cover: Matthew Dix of North Tabor Farm at the Farmers Market. *Courtesy of Joyce Dresser*.

First published 2024

Manufactured in the United States

ISBN 9781467157643

Library of Congress Control Number: 2024931855

Dedicated to the memories of
Shannon (Gregory) Carbone and Waylon Madison Sauer,
two Vineyarders who left us before their time.

CONTENTS

Foreword, by Marnely Murray   9
Prologue   11
Acknowledgements   15

1. Native American Staples   17
2. Colonial Cuisine   27
3. From the Sea   37
4. Portuguese Specialties   45
5. African American Selections   53
6. Ethnic Options   61
7. Seasonal Treats   67
8. Foraging and Gleaning   75
9. The Farmers Market   85
10. Remember?   91
11. Beverages   117
12. Just Desserts   127
13. Sweets   131
14. Island Grown Initiative   139
15. Historic Restaurants   145

Epilogue   175
Notes   177
Selected Bibliography   185
Index   187
Authors' Notes   189

FOREWORD

*M*artha's Vineyard, an island seven miles off the coast of Massachusetts, is truly a testament to the diversity of cultures that have graced its shores. Within the Island, a remarkable culinary history unfolds—one of community, resilience, and traditions.

In this inviting book, we embark on a culinary journey through time, tracing the gastronomic footprints left by generations past and present on this island. Where will this journey take you? As you turn the pages, you'll create your own culinary map of the Island that will deliver not only delicious treasures but also a full understanding of what makes up the way Martha's Vineyard eats and drinks.

We'll dive into Martha's Vineyard's culinary record and uncover the true essence of the Island's sustenance—its rich recipes simmered in tradition and the vibrant culinary efforts that showcase Martha's Vineyard's broad heritage.

Nestled amid the magical fishing village of Menemsha, the serene landscapes of Chilmark, the vibrant kitchens of Oak Bluffs, the dining tables of Edgartown, the Vineyard Haven eateries, the farmers markets of West Tisbury, and the fields of Aquinnah are the souls of the culinary customs of the Island. From the Indigenous Wampanoag people to the arrival of the eastern European students, the Portuguese specialties, the melting pot of the African selections, and the blend of Italian, Brazilian, Jamaican, and Asian options, the variety served on the Island today truly makes up the Island food tapestry. The pages of this book look to celebrate this diversity while honoring those before us and looking toward the future flavors.

Here, you'll come to discover the voices of renowned chefs and cooks, of local farmers, fishermen, foragers, cheese mongers, and overall stewards of the land as they chronicle the symbiotic relationship between the land and the sea. Whether it's evoking a sense of nostalgia (if you've lived on Martha's Vineyard for decades) or a sense of wonder (if you're visiting for the first time), the one feeling I'm sure this tome will evoke is that of hunger and delight as we discover a world of enticing bites.

Beyond the kitchen, this book shines a light on the importance of Martha's Vineyard as a hub for sustainable living. It features the vibrant farm-to-table movement, showcasing the Island's commitment to sourcing fresh, locally grown produce and sustainable seafood, a true testament to the community's appreciation for the environment and its bounty. From the West Tisbury Farmers Market to the local foraging and gleaning, coming together with our very own Island Grown Initiative, you'll discover there's more to the Island than its pristine beaches.

Savor these anecdotes, recipes, and stories—drink up the essence of Martha's Vineyard's culinary past, present, and future. May this book be your dining invitation to join the Island's culinary history, foster a deeper appreciation for the delightful flavors, and enrich your lives with the ingredients that make up the fabric of the Island.

Marnely Murray
Pastry chef and marketer at Shored Up Digital

PROLOGUE

When Joyce and I began to write *A Culinary History of Martha's Vineyard*, we knew we were in for a good time. Who doesn't like to eat? Who doesn't talk about food? Who doesn't enjoy tidbits on Vineyard eateries?

We sampled ethnic cuisines. We tried different breakfast dishes. We uncovered unusual elements in the Vineyard's dining history. And we enjoyed hand pies and patties along the way.

We've gleaned the fields and chopped the veggies for church suppers. Our son-in-law is a chef. And we love to eat. Isn't that sufficient criteria to write a book about Vineyard dining?

In June 2023, Heather Seger, executive director of the Martha's Vineyard Museum, initiated Martha's Vineyard Flavors, because, as she put it, "Food is so universal. It's something everyone can connect to."

Dr. Jessica Harris opened the food history symposium. Dr. Harris is the author of *The Martha's Vineyard Table*, which, according to the *Vineyard Gazette*, "solidified her Island fame, becoming a Bible of sorts for devout Vineyard eaters." Dr. Harris described her book on Island food as "from the highbrow to the down 'n dirty."

The symposium ranged from Juli Vanderhoop discussing Native Americans foraging to Rebecca Haag expounding on Island Grown Initiative: the means to meet the Island's food challenges.

Marnely Murray, a panelist, reported, "The event was well done and organized, truly a great experience for all who attended and participated!"[1]

Laurie Howick of Oak Bluffs noted the speakers were both informative and inspirational. She wrote in an email, "Great work is being done on this Island to educate future generations, feed all who are in need, preserve traditional methods of growing and harvesting the bounty around us, and promote thoughtfulness in all aspects of food production, preparation, distribution, and waste/refuse systems."[2]

The Museum is to be commended for bringing food to the fore. Food flourishes in so many ways on Martha's Vineyard we feel this book justifies its existence. A culinary history is a useful tool to explore past and present restaurants and discuss a range of food issues on Island. This book delivers a healthy serving of dietary discussions on the history of food on Martha's Vineyard. We live on an isle of plenty, yet sharing the bounty is a challenge.

Locally sourced vegetables and grains, such as Turkey Red Winter Wheat and ancient Wampanoag corn, are grown and harvested in fields across the Island. Cattle, sheep, pigs, and chickens are raised and slaughtered for local consumption. Shellfish are harvested from the waters of coastal shores and ponds, and fish are caught from the streams, ponds, and ocean. Deer hunting is critical to curtail the burgeoning deer population. Geese, ducks, and wild turkeys may be hunted in autumn. With myriad food sources, in the air, on land, and sea, Martha's Vineyard enjoys a modicum of self-sufficiency. Locally raised food is shared through the Island Food Pantry, the Farmers Market, and restaurants across the Vineyard.

Restaurants allow us to sample and savor our favorite foods without getting our hands dirty or following a recipe. Over the last century, dozens of restaurants have flourished across the Vineyard. We rekindle memories of a few notable eateries over the years. Remember the Kapigan? Blueberry Hill? The Captain's Table?

Our final chapter covers restaurants still flourishing after a half century. Giordano's and the Black Dog have an extensive following; do you know when the Home Port opened? Where did the ArtCliff come from? How far back does the Ocean View go? We credit owners, family, and staff in the kitchen as well as the front of the house for keeping the business flourishing through years of staffing issues, ferry strikes, hurricanes, fires, floods, financial meltdowns, and other catastrophes.

When Joyce feeds Kutter, our Miniature Schnauzer, she always calls out "Mangia, Mangia," Italian for "Eat, Eat!" *Photo by Joyce Dresser.*

Running a restaurant is not an easy business, although the staff make it look that way.

Finally, this project is a work in progress, a snapshot in time. Any one of the historic restaurants could close tomorrow. Ownership changes, management decisions, and diners' desires differ from year to year; what was popular last year falls from favor this. Our culinary history encompasses the past to inform the present and prognosticate the future.

Now, sit back and savor the luxury and variety of the Vineyard's culinary delights.

ACKNOWLEDGEMENTS

*A*ppropriately, we set up shop on the dining table to write this book, following the well-honed recipe of historical nonfiction, starting at the beginning and ending at the end.

Along the way, like the *Phantom Gourmet*, we sought culinary advice from Vineyard chefs, staff, and customers. Librarian Hilary Wallcox of the *Vineyard Gazette* shared arcane culinary articles. Bow Van Riper at the Martha's Vineyard Museum knows his Vineyard history. Oak Bluffs librarians generously loaned requested books. Restaurateurs shared their skills, secrets, and stories.

Frances Finnegan suggested the gospel of Louise Tate King's *The Martha's Vineyard Cook Book*. Islanders shared memories of favorite eateries. We thank Carol Meikle for her images of Jamaican food and suggesting Caribbean cuisine. We enjoyed interviews with Kerry Alley, Jan Burhman, Lisa and Winston Christie, Virginia Coutinho, Charlie Esposito, Buster Giordano, both Brion McGroartys, Marjorie Peirce, Robin Rebello Meader, Todd Rebello, Chef Deon Thomas, Andrea Trindade, and Julie Vanderhoop. We even invited Bing, the Google AI guy, but found he wasn't always up to speed.

We garnish each chapter with an unusual dietary dilemma at the beginning and spice each chapter's end with a memorable meal, Joyce on odd-numbered chapters, Tom on even.

This project has been frosted and baked by the professionals at The History Press. We appreciate the expertise of Mike Kinsella, acquisitions editor; Abigail Fleming, our superb copy editor; Dani McGrath, marketeer supreme; Maddison Potter, senior publicist; and Samantha Linnane, author sales, which is what this is all about.

Now it is ready to be served.

Bon Appétit

1

NATIVE AMERICAN STAPLES

Piles of seashells (called middens) along Squibnocket Pond in Aquinnah are a reminder that Native American forbears lived on Martha's Vineyard thousands of years ago. The middens indicate the pond was once an arm of the ocean, as the shells matured in seawater.

*P*eople of the First Light, the Wampanoag, have hunted and gathered on Martha's Vineyard for thousands of years. Bones from whitetail deer attest to the Native Americans' skill in hunting. Drift whales were a source of food, as the legendary ancestor Moshup shared with his people. A hunter could kill a deer or catch a flounder, which puts food on the table. Foraging plants, roots, and berries continues to be part of the Indian heritage. A gatherer can collect chestnuts or blueberries and enjoy found food.

In prehistory, humans were basically hunter-gatherers: foraging, fishing, and hunting for food. That was how we ate.[3]

Initially, Martha's Vineyard was part of Cape Cod, with dry land connecting the land masses. When the last of the glaciers melted, the sea level rose dramatically, severing the Vineyard from the Cape, leaving the Native Americans either in Mashpee or Aquinnah. And that was how life began on Noepe, the Wampanoag word for Martha's Vineyard, "land amid the waters." That is the prehistory of the Wampanoag, who settled the Vineyard before it became an island about 3000 BC.

In the early years, no one was a food producer, a farmer. Farming was neither invented nor discovered but evolved over time by people who copied food producers. A hunter-gatherer who dabbled in planting seeds and appreciating his harvest gradually shifted his focus to farming. Farming requires dedication, tending, and protecting a site. And patience, waiting for the harvest. Hunting or gathering produces immediate results. Or nothing.

Jared Diamond, author of *Guns, Germs, and Steel*, explains the origins of class, based on where early man got his food. "The people of areas with a head start on food production gained a head start on the path leading toward guns, germs, and steel. The result was a long series of collisions between the haves and have-nots of history."[4]

Agriculture arrived on Martha's Vineyard within the last thousand years, with corn reaching the Northeast around AD 900, followed by beans. Squash evolved about the same time. Natives farmed these staples to supplement their seafood, hunting, and foraging.

Today we honor the Native people who work the land, respect the land, and share the land. Landownership was not part of the Native American conceit; it was instituted by English colonists who settled the Vineyard in the 1640s, imposing their culture, religion, laws, customs, and mores on the Native Islanders.

Juli Vanderhoop, a Wampanoag woman, spoke at the Food Symposium held at the Martha's Vineyard Museum. Growing up in Gay Head/Aquinnah, she foraged in the woods and fields near her home. "As the last child of my family…when we walked all over Aquinnah, I found myself as a five- or six-year-old dragging behind them," she said. "I'd drink from the streams. The smells would rise around me and help me find the deepest part [of the water]. I lagged behind and found the berries, the sassafras, to nourish me to bring me home."

When discussing foraging, finding wild foods in the woods and fields around us, Juli acknowledged that as a little girl, she was more concerned with keeping up with her older brothers than the found food along the woodland path.

What Juli learned as a child colors what she does today. Foraging walks are part of the Wampanoag credo, sharing the native plants that flourish on Martha's Vineyard. Wild edible foods inform current diets, but one must know how to find them, when they grow, where they proliferate and how to use them. Foraging is an educational experience.

In their introduction to *The Martha's Vineyard Cook Book*, authors Louise Tate King and Jean Stewart Wexler recognized the influence of local Native Americans on current (1970) dietary options. "Today's Vineyarders draw on an expanded heritage in preparing their meals. Some of their recipes, like a simple but satisfying cornmeal mush (called Hasty Pudding) were used by the Wampanoag Indians who hunted and trapped amongst the riches of the Island long before the white man moved in."[5]

Cranberry Day is recognized in Aquinnah. When the bogs are harvested, the cranberries are dried and used in jams, jellies, breads, cakes, and more. The cranberry bogs in Aquinnah are on the Lobsterville Road. And there are bogs on Lambert's Cove Road, under the jurisdiction of the Vineyard Open Land Facility, gleaned by the Island Grown Initiative.

The history of the Wampanoag links hunter-gatherers to food producers. Jared Diamond explained the "sharp divide between nomadic hunger-gatherers and sedentary food producers." Gradually, the tribe did both, foraging and hunting, as well as tending crops, as the Wampanoag do today.

Diamond continued, describing a misconception of "a distinction between food producers as active managers of their land and hunter-gatherers as mere collectors of the land's wild produce." Hunters who burned underbrush encouraged growth of edible plants, an element of farming. Also, clearing brush made it easier to spot small game. Again, the Wampanoag are active managers of the landscape, whether hunting, fishing, foraging, or farming. They do it all.[6]

In her autobiographical cookbook *High on the Hog*, Dr. Jessica Harris recounts a trip to Aquinnah: "As the road entered the town, through the trees I saw a huge stone beehive oven behind a massive pile of firewood." For first-time visitors, the imposing oven indicates an intriguing experience. The site is the workplace of Juli Vanderhoop's Orange Peel Bakery. The oven "was part of a new local bakery where we were all to meet. I was curious about the gathering. It was not a powwow or tribal event; rather it was a group of local families and their friends coming together for pizza night." Dr. Harris was captivated by this culinary and social adventure.[7]

Juli Vanderhoop earned the Creative Living Award in 2023. *Courtesy of the Martha's Vineyard Times.*

After explaining how everyone brings a topping for their pizza, as well as their own beverage, Dr. Harris introduced Juli Vanderhoop, the daughter of a Wampanoag family, who invited her community to share the bounty of food she bakes in her imposing stone oven. Juli's culinary talents match her social standing, welcoming the town to her doorstep in a cheerful gathering, working together, and enjoying a meal with strangers. In high praise, Dr. Harris observed, "That fall evening on Martha's Vineyard, I was struck by the seamless way that the assembled folk came together over food—sharing, preparing, celebrating, and for the duration of the evening, melding into an extended family."

The community pizza program at Orange Peel continues to bring people together and feed them.

Juli opened her Orange Peel Bakery in 2007. She does more than host the ever-popular pizza nights; she thrives on making food for Islanders. Growing up in Aquinnah, with her mother baking innumerable pies, Juli recalled, "I fell in love with food and the oven. The smell. There is so much joy in food. It can be an inward process or out. When I had kids, I didn't want my kids to eat junk. So, I started baking for them. Everything we do here at the bakery is handmade."

The name Orange Peel refers to Juli's recollection of her grandmother boiling orange peels in sugar water, then setting them out to dry on the windowsill to make candy. The aroma and taste are a sweet memory.

The best way to market a restaurant is to serve good food, food that deserves a return visit. That keeps business going. Juli's mother, Anne, taught her that. By making good food, you don't have to advertise as much; people will return for more. Juli promotes Orange Peel Bakery through her friendly manner and informative conversation. She knows it's a long drive up-Island to the bakery for a loaf of bread, but she sings the praises of Aquinnah. "I want people to come here and eat from the ground. To know that their food comes from under their feet."

During Covid, Juli was among the first to adapt to a socially distanced status with curbside pickup. Customers got their baked goods without interacting with anyone. Orange Peel set an example for the community. Juli said, "The community was responding to me. That makes me feel so much better." Instead of being taken for granted, Juli feels recognized and rewarded by the local support of Orange Peel.

Juli's goal in opening Orange Peel was "to uphold this place for people to come." And people have come. The bakery thrives on the honor system, as it is not always staffed. Customers leave money or pay on Venmo. Juli trusts the community, but she did install cameras. She "trusts her neighbors and friends." And that is Juli's credo: she is part of the community and feels the community trusts her in return.

Hiring help and housing for staff are challenges in running Juli's micro-bakery. She needs staff so she doesn't overwork herself.

Juli's mother, Anne, married William Vanderhoop in 1949. The Vanderhoops had seven children: Buddy, Ricky, David, Todd (passed at age two), Cully, Chip, and Juli.

Anne and William divorced in 1970; a decade later, Anne married Luther Madison. He became her pie partner, making the filling while she baked the crust. Luther taught Juli his culinary expertise; she refers to her stepfather as "the pie-guy," with a smile. Luther and Anne Vanderhoop baked myriad pies over the years for the Aquinnah Shop Restaurant. That was Juli's culinary family.

Wampanoag culinary culture embraces the three sisters: beans, corn, and squash. These innocuous vegetables work together, like family, sisters with a mutual goal of a bountiful harvest. They support one another when planted together. It is suggested to plant corn in

The beehive fieldstone oven is the centerpiece of Orange Peel Bakery, where community pizza is baked. *Photo by Joyce Dresser.*

For decades, Anne Vanderhoop and Luther Madison were pie partners at the Aquinnah Shop. Their banana cream pies were memorable. *Courtesy of the* Vineyard Gazette.

hills, with beans around them, and squash scattered about. Beans climb corn stalks. Squash provide shade, which reduces the need for water. And when the soil gets less sunlight, there are fewer weeds. It's a win-win-win program, part of Native American agriculture for generations.[8]

Jared Diamond, in *Guns, Grains, and Steel*, suggested that eastern Native Americans adopted crops from Mexico in their agricultural efforts.

Diamond elaborated on the evolution of the three sisters. Natives domesticated squash on their own, but "Mexican crops finally began to reach the eastern United States by trade routes after AD 1. Corn arrived around AD 200, but its role remained very minor for many centuries. Finally, around AD 900 a new variety of corn adapted to North America's short summers appeared, and the arrival of beans around AD 1100 completed Mexico's crop trinity of corn, beans, and squash. Eastern U.S. farming became greatly intensified."[9]

The three sisters gradually entered the lexicon of staples in the Wampanoag diet, providing a bountiful, generous harvest. So, although the Wampanoag trace their time on the Vineyard to 8000 BC, it has only been in the last millennium that the three sisters produced the agricultural bounty enjoyed today.

There are innumerable variations in preparing corn, beans, and squash, but one recipe meets the needs of a decolonized diet, based on plants without sugar, dairy, or gluten. Such a diet is sought because it combats Lyme disease by reducing inflammation. It affects diabetes by cutting levels of glucose. And a decolonized diet both improves athletic capability and enhances sleep levels.

Squash, beans, and corn together create a nutritious diet. Combining complex carbohydrates, fatty acids, and complementary amino acids creates a complete protein. Like three sisters, together in a family, each vegetable contributes its strength. The whole is greater than the individuals.

A Three Sister Salad is called a confetti salad where everything is chopped in a small dice.

1 medium-sized red onion
2 jalapeños, finely chopped
1 red pepper
1 green pepper
1 pound cooked lima beans or fava beans
3 ears corn
1 large Hubbard, 2 acorn, or several pattypan squash
1–3 tablespoons butter
1–3 tablespoons olive oil
Fresh or dried sage and thyme. If fresh, a handful of each finely chopped
1–3 teaspoons cumin
Cayenne (to taste), but if not sure, start with 1/8 teaspoon
Salt
Pepper

Grill (or roast) 3 ears of corn on a flame until they are a little scorched. Allow to cool and cut the kernels from the cob.

Melt 2 tablespoons of butter and 2 tablespoons of olive oil together in a large sauté pan. Add the squash. Cook over high heat for about 5–7 minutes. Turn down and toss in the herbs, spices, salt, and pepper. Add more butter and olive oil if necessary. The aim here is to not make a mash with the squash but to create more of a home-fry consistency. So do not over stir or push on the cubes. Allow the squash to get golden and crisp on the outside and tender on the inside.

When the squash is done, mix all the ingredients together in a large bowl. Taste. Maybe add more salt or a little more pepper. We like to balance the salad with a peach-infused balsamic vinegar and a little more olive oil. Of course, all of this can and should be adjusted to one's taste. If spice is not your thing, you can use or lose the jalapeño and add more savory herbs. This is just a basic structure and approach to a salad that is flexible. It can be served while the squash is still warm or cold. The Three Sisters are such a complement to each other that they can serve as the foundation for so many flavors.[10]

Juli Vanderhoop described a program she uses to train ethnic chefs in her kitchen. When she thought about where our food comes from, she wanted to work with other chefs. "The highlight is on food we don't have here," she said, "ingredients not found in our kitchen."

She opened her bakery to chefs from the Philippines, Panama, and Jamaica, combining people and place. She lets them tell their story, do their thing. They work in her kitchen, and she highlights their food. Juli wants to share her expertise with others as well as learn from them.

Private chefs use her kitchen and work on their own. For two years, Juli mentored Canieka Fleming of the Loud Kitchen at the Ritz Café. They have a great relationship. "I do whatever I can do to help," she said.

Juli shared Outer Known, a program that recognizes Orange Peel as a small business helping the community in a big way. Outer Known produces ethically focused clothing, a brand focused on sustainability. "It was a real compliment to get their support," Juli said. Using organically sourced product, and including Juli in the design, Outer Known manufactured orange T-shirts for the bakery. This worthy program puts Orange Peel on a wider map.

Vineyarders have become hunter-gatherers of Orange Peel's baked goods, goods that come from the soil through the hands of Juli Vanderhoop.

A new face has appeared in Aquinnah. Del Araujo, a member of the Wampanoag tribe, and his wife, Jennifer Straub, opened Aquila on the Cliffs in 2022. Aquila offers a variety of coffee drinks and snacks as well as Native Island art. The name Aquila refers to the constellation of an eagle, seen overhead in the summer sky.

Not limited to Aquila, Araujo serves treats at the Sharks baseball games, handles the museum's dietary needs,eeeee and is a dining delight for healthy Vineyarders at the Y. This is one busy couple!

One of my favorite dishes is baked stuffed shrimp. In the early years of my first marriage, I decided to make it for Sunday dinner. It turned out a little strange, as I didn't realize I was supposed to peel off the shrimp's shell and butterfly it. Somehow, we ate it.

2

COLONIAL CUISINE

The Beatrice House stood by the Arcade off Circuit Avenue. In the 1920s, an off-Island choir sang at the Tabernacle and dined at the Beatrice House, getting three meals a day for ten dollars a week.

*T*n the early days, there were no hotels, restaurants, or bars on Martha's Vineyard.

Towns incorporated in seventeenth-century Massachusetts were required to offer a place for a traveler to spend the night. They had to provide a bite to eat for people traveling through their town. Thus, taverns sprang up throughout colonial Massachusetts. By 1656, virtually every town provided such a facility for people journeying through.

There was nothing special about these taverns; they were quite common, ordinary, if you will. In fact, a tavern was referred to as an "ordinary" in colonial America.

There were only three towns on Martha's Vineyard until the late nineteenth century: Edgartown, Tisbury, and Chilmark. Edgartown and Tisbury had ordinaries, but in Chilmark there were few visitors because of inadequate roadways. By 1700, local men were licensed as innkeepers. Several Tiltons, Cottles, and Mayhews appear on tavern licenses in eighteenth-century Chilmark. Across the Sound in Falmouth, the first tavern opened in 1665.

In colonial days, even on the Vineyard—with its small population and limited access—taverns were the only source of sustenance for travelers. Unless visitors knew someone in town, they would seek food and lodging at a local tavern. Class structure was imposed from the start in colonial America. Women, Blacks, and Native Americans were not welcome to stay at a tavern or ordinary.

The tavern became a social setting to meet other men. With limited sites to become acquainted with new people, the tavern evolved into a gathering place for locals to meet visitors and visitors to learn about the community.

Regarding alcohol, the innkeeper held one license for beer and wine and a second for hard or strong liquor. Food and sustenance were part of the tavern's function, but the quality and quantity of food and drink depended on the innkeeper's talents and supplies. Meals in local taverns ranged from delicious to inconsistent to putrid. It depended on the innkeeper, what was on hand, and their proficiency behind the stove. Taverns served alcohol, often brewed on site.

Hard cider was frequently available. An apple crop would not last the winter but could be squeezed into apple cider. Barrels could be stored, transported, and sold as a stimulating beverage.

Because the Vineyard was a British colony, tea was ever-present. The apocryphal origin of Tea Lane dates to the pre-Revolutionary era. Angry at the tax Parliament levied on tea and desirous of their beloved drink, Chilmark residents sent a Captain Leonard to London. He filled his vessel with tea and returned to the Vineyard, where he smuggled the tea into his aunt's basement on the eponymous Tea Lane. The good captain avoided the taxman and shared his ill-gotten beverage with neighbor, family, and friend.

If a traveler were in a hurry, the original fast food, a sandwich, was offered. Mince pie was another quick meal. Hand-held like a sandwich, the meat or fruit was wrapped in dough and cooked. When a guest asked for one, the pie would be reheated.

One of the first tavernkeepers of record in Edgartown was William Weeks, who held a license in 1681 or earlier. Numerous taverns flourished in the county seat, especially along North Water Street. The Kelley House opened as a tavern in 1748. It was known as the Marcy House in the 1800s and then reverted to the Kelley House in the twentieth century. Daniel Webster stayed at what is now the Edgartown Inn, then the Gibbs House.

One place that links the past with the present was the Daggett House, also on North Water Street. Now a private home, this legendary hostelry

Orange Peel Bakery sells hand pies, pastry filled with fruit, similar to what colonial taverns sold to guests on the go. *Photo by Joyce Dresser.*

dates to the early 1700s, with a reputation for food and lodging that survived the generations. It became a private dwelling in 2005.

A loyal patron recalled, "At the Daggett House, Deb and I loved the grape nut bread/toast. We were in the room right above the kitchen one stay and the aroma of the baking bread would wake us up at 6 am every morning, not a bad way to start the day."[11]

Isaac Chase was licensed to operate a tavern in Holmes Hole (now Vineyard Haven) in 1677 not far from Water Street. Besides running his hostel, Chase ran the Falmouth ferry, which sailed down the Bass River (now Water Street) and docked at what we know as Five Corners. As with many such establishments, innkeeping passed from father to son, from Isaac, to Thomas, to Abraham.

Also in Holmes Hole was Allen's Tavern. In the Revolutionary era, Sarah Chase Daggett Allen was the tavernkeeper. The mother of ten, Sarah would have been quite attuned to the current political climate, according to Nora Van Riper, a historical reenactor. Timothy and Jane Luce operated a tavern at what is now the Mansion House on Main Street.

Robert Cathcart managed a tavern in West Tisbury in 1701. Known as Kithcarts, it stood on Brandy Brow, "named for the liquor that flowed at this 19th century establishment and for the geologic feature on which it stood," not far from the Mill Pond, on the left, going into town.[12]

The only public houses in Oak Bluffs were in the Eastville section of Cottage City, as the town was known prior to 1907. Chandlery shops sold ship supplies. Taverns along the harbor awaited crew from ships, anxious for a drink or a meal. Sailors often had to wait for repairs or supplies for their vessel; they bunked at a nearby tavern or hostel. It was a rough, seafaring

THE CLAGHORN TAVERN,
BUILT ABOUT 1730.
NOW THE OLIVER LINTON HOUSE.

Claghorn Tavern was licensed to Joseph Claghorn. Revolutionary captain John Paul Jones stayed at the Claghorn in the 1770s. And Polly Daggett Hillman, one of the liberty pole ladies, worked at the Claghorn. *From Charles Banks's* History of Martha's Vineyard.

community where brothels and pirates flourished, often without fear of restriction or retribution, a Barbary coast on Martha's Vineyard.

In Gay Head/Aquinnah, because virtually no transients ventured so far in the off-season, there was no call for a tavern or inn. In the summer, local families offered short-term lodging for those visitors who remained overnight in Gay Head.

The local tavern, whether in Edgartown, Chilmark, or Tisbury, usually made a big deal over breakfast. Selections ranged from steak, sausages, and bacon, to fish, eggs, bread, and coffee and, of course, tea. Midafternoon lunch would be served, something light, but filling, like a sandwich or hand pie. A hearty meal or supper, like a chicken and oyster stifle (see page 32), could be expected in the evening.

Chicken was served frequently, as chickens were plentiful in colonial homesteads: easy to raise and feed and quick to serve. Pork was popular, as it could be stored for some time. High-end taverns, such as those on North Water Street in Edgartown or Main Street in Holmes Hole, often served beef, oysters, or veal.

Potted meats were popular. Potting meant boiling or baking a piece of meat until it was tender. Step two would be to pound it with a wooden mallet, or beetle, to mash it into a paste, adding spices and fat. The paste was then poured into an earthenware jar, topped with melted butter, and sealed with melted fat. Caveaching was a similar technique for fish: fry the fish in oil, pickle with vinegar, and then seal with oil. Such techniques were successful for storing fish and meats for an extended period, especially when the weather was cold. When the tavernkeeper opened the jar, the meaty paste was ready to be spread on bread for a sandwich.

Joseph Chase Allen, crusty reporter for the *Vineyard Gazette*, advocated a cast iron frying pan as the very best utensil for a New England chef. He assured anyone who would listen that the cast iron pan gave the food a better flavor. His grandmother made baking powder biscuits in an iron frying pan on top of the stove.

Like most Europeans, the British measured ingredients by weight, with scales. This was time consuming. Colonists adapted the system of measuring by cup and spoon, a faster, easier way to measure ingredients.

The Beatrice House was near the Arcade on Circuit Avenue. It was popular with guests at the Campground, offering meals and lodging. *Courtesy of the Oak Bluffs Library.*

A meal could be prepared using salt pork as a base, adding beans, potatoes, and onions, with a bit of cornmeal. Combinations of ingredients served as a base for many a hearty, healthy winter meal in colonial days. Adding jelly or pickles, canned in the summer, added zing to sparse winter meals.

The following partial recipes offer a few colonial delights to whet your culinary curiosity. Recipes are from the 1971 edition of *The Martha's Vineyard Cook Book* by Louise Tate King and Jean Stewart Wexler.

Chicken and Oyster Stifle

This was a popular colonial dish, albeit bearing a somewhat arcane name. The word stifle refers to the means of cooking the chicken, literally smothering it. Cover the chicken, browning, then braising it in a seasoned, thickened sauce to tenderize the meat. Spread a quart of fresh drained oysters over the casserole and cook another 15 minutes, until the oysters curl. Remove from the oven, pour the sauce over it all, and serve on a heated platter.

Potato Bargain

This dining delight was a go-to meal in winter when the root cellar was devoid of salvageable vegetables other than potatoes and onions. Start with diced salt pork in a covered iron skillet; remove and repeat with sliced onions. Return the salt pork and add sliced potatoes, and boiling water to just cover the ingredients; cook slowly.

According to the Tilton family recipe, a good bargain uses minimal water, cooking slowly, and allows steam to do the cooking. Welcome Tilton, sailing the *Alice B. Wentworth*, observed, "better after two or three days but tiresome after a week of being served up daily."[13]

Red Flannel Hash

This concoction was created from left overs to make a tasty dish that stands on its own. Bring together salt pork, chopped potatoes, onions, garlic, and beets, with a clove of garlic and a sprig of celery. The beets provide the color for the dish's name.

Clam Stifle

A recipe for Clam Stifle was published by the *Vineyard Gazette* in 1921 but neglected to include proportions of various ingredients. It was assumed any competent cook would know how much to use.

The recipe calls for a quart of clams, separating ribs from stomach. Layer with potatoes, another layer of scallions and a third of clams; repeat, using all the clams. Add a half pint of milk and as much butter, "that your conscience will let you use." Cover with salt pork slices and bake two hours.

Puddings

Wheat and oats were a challenge to grow on the Vineyard, so colonists resorted to corn, which makes a tasty pudding. For those on the run, it could be cooked and served quickly, hence a "hasty pudding."

Corn meal was the primary ingredient of johnny cake, a bread-like pancake. It could be heated or not, devoured quickly, moving the traveler on.

Pumpkin Pie

The use of pumpkin in a pie was often interchangeable with squash, or even gourds. Adding apples to pumpkin soup made it richer; with sherry and cream one had an elegant repast.

Apple Muffins

These muffins were included in a recipe from Annie Lord's cooking class at the First Baptist Church in Vineyard Haven, in 1912. It's a muffin recipe that includes a cup of chopped or coarsely grated apples.

Baked Indian Pudding

The "Indian" part of this pudding is the cornmeal. If you're cooking your pudding on the Island, why not slice some windfall apples from a roadside tree into the baking dish?

8 portions
3 tablespoons butter
⅔ cup dark molasses
5 cups milk
¾ teaspoon cinnamon
¾ teaspoon nutmeg
½ teaspoon ginger (optional)
½ cup yellow cornmeal
½ teaspoon salt
6 tablespoons sugar
Heavy or whipped cream or vanilla ice cream

Preheat oven to 300 degrees. Grease a baking dish, about 8x10 inches and at least 3 inches deep.

In a saucepan heat the butter, molasses, and 4 cups of the milk. In another saucepan, thoroughly combine the spices, cornmeal, salt, and sugar. Then stir in the heated milk mixture. Cook over moderate heat, stirring frequently, until it thickens. Pour into the baking dish. Add the remaining cup of milk, but do not stir it in.

Bake at least 3 hours without stirring. Serve warm with heavy cream, whipped cream, or a scoop of rich vanilla ice cream.[14]

Sea Voyage Gingerbread
Published in the Vineyard Gazette *of August 28, 1857*

Sift two pounds of flour into a pan and cut up in it a pound and a quarter of fresh butter: rub the butter well into the flour then mix in a pint of West Indian molasses and a pound of the best brown sugar.

Beat eight eggs until very light. Stir into the eggs two glasses of a gill of brandy: add also to the eggs a teacup full of ground ginger and a tablespoon of powdered cinnamon with a teaspoon of soda melted in a little warm water. Wet the flour, etc. with this mixture till it becomes a soft dough.

Sprinkle a little flour on your paste board, and with a broad knife spread portions of the mixture thickly and smoothly upon it. The thickness must be equal all through; therefore, spread it carefully and evenly, as the dough will be too soft to roll out. Then with the edge of a tumbler dipped in flour, cut it out into round cakes.

Have square pans, slightly buttered; lay the cakes in them sufficiently far apart to prevent their running into each other when baked. Set the pans into a brick oven and bake the cakes well, seeing that they do not burn.

These cakes will keep during a long voyage and are frequently carried to sea. Many persons find highly spiced gingerbread a preventive to seasickness.[15]

Islanders prepared for winter by laying in a supply of foods stored in root cellars. With food in short supply and winter weather limiting access to supplies, Vineyarders hunted deer, rabbits, and small game. Oysters, frozen in sawdust, would last for weeks. Ice fishing at Tisbury Great Pond was a common activity.

In his 1963 book *It Began with a Whale*, John Daggett recalled, "We never worried about the winter weather, but took it in stride because we usually had pork, bacon, chickens, eggs, and also vegetables in the cellar. We always had a barrel of flour, another of sugar, and usually one or two of apples, as well as a hundred pounds of prunes."[16]

First Vineyard meal, 1995. Chili? Really.

The backstory: Joyce and I went to high school together in Holden, Massachusetts, but were not a couple. We re-met at our thirtieth reunion. Joyce invited me down to the Vineyard for a weekend. I accepted. She cooked a vegetarian chili. I loved it. I fell in love with her. And the Vineyard.

3

FROM THE SEA

When one considers Oysters Rockefeller, it is assumed the Rockefellers were creative chefs. Not so. When you think about it…the Vineyard version, Quahogs Rockefeller, is also a very rich dish.

*R*egardless of the hazards of the weather, commercialization, and pollution, people still crave food from the sea. As hunter-gatherers, humans learned to fish, harvest clams and shellfish, and survive with the fortunes found in the ocean.

Seafood recipes abound, describing how to catch it and cook it and the delights of eating lobster, clams, quahogs, shrimp, bluefish, swordfish, cod, and schrod.

Today it's always a magical experience to pull food right out of the ocean. There's still mystery in the deep.

For years, whaling ships sailed the seas searching for and capturing whales for their oil. Life aboard ship was boring, tedious, and repetitive, except when a whale was sighted. Then life got exciting.

The role of the cook was to keep the crew content with decent food. That was not easy before refrigeration. When a ship stopped in a Vineyard harbor for supplies, Island meats like poultry, mutton, or beef were loaded aboard. Vegetables such as corn or potatoes and grains like rye could be purchased to meet the crew's culinary needs.

A reliable source of sustenance was hardtack, which is just what it sounds like: hard. It was baked on Island, then loaded aboard ship for the whaling journey. Because it was dry, it lasted a long time, as long as it didn't get wet.

Flour, water, and salt were the ingredients of hardtack. Basically, it was just a hard biscuit. Whalemen dunked their rations in coffee to soften them up. Hardtack could be added to soup or stew, occasionally fried with bacon—anything to excite a bland, hard, cracker.

Dr. Daniel Fisher set up a hardtack bakery on his wharf in Edgartown in the mid-1800s, today's Old Sculpin Gallery. He leased farmland in West Tisbury and hired farmers to grow wheat, which was ground at his mill on North Road. To complete the project, he built a roadway, linking nine miles of cart roads from his mill to Edgartown. Today, that route is known as the Dr. Fisher Road.

Besides hardtack, whalemen were treated to salt pork and beans or potatoes. When the opportunity arose, crew would catch fresh fish, sea turtles, or dolphin. Fruit was a luxury; whalemen had a minimal amount of calcium in their diet. In short, the whaleman's diet was boring, lacking in sufficient nutrients, and unhealthy. That was the way it was.

In his introduction to the *Martha's Vineyard Cook Book*, Henry Beetle Hough, editor of the *Vineyard Gazette*, credited Vineyarders with their maritime prowess in harnessing the commercial draw of swordfish. In the 1920s, no one seemed to have heard of swordfish. By 1970, everyone doted on swordfish.

During the Depression, Edgartown swordfishermen did not feel the pinch of deprivation. They harvested their seafaring crop, trading with Boston restaurants whose customers craved the fish and had the money to pay for it. Swordfish grew more popular, which meant more money for Edgartown swordfishermen. It was a win-win situation for everyone, except the swordfish. Hough gave Vineyard fishermen full credit for spreading the word.

Up-Islanders survived the Depression better than many Vineyarders because they could fish, farm, and hunt for their meals. And Vineyard waters offer an abundance of saltwater fish besides swordfish; think bluefish, false albacore, flounder, and striped bass.

Eldridge's Fish Market, in Edgartown, separated the lower Main Street shops from the bustling waterfront, filled with sailors and ships coming and

Jay Lagemann designed this statue of a swordfisherman for the 300th anniversary of the town of Chilmark, in 1994. It overlooks Menemsha Beach. *Photo by Joyce Dresser.*

going. The Fish Market opened about 1925 and was sold to the Yacht Club in 1966, a forty-year reign.

The Market was a site for old men to gather and retell tall tales of the sea. Yes, the fishermen shared fish tales but also memories of manager John Correia, who began working at the Market shortly after it opened and continued until it closed.

In the early years of the Depression, it felt like scallops were limitless; the ships, sheds, and shanties were overwhelmed. Bags of scallops were stacked around the Market awaiting shucking, and the shuckers often prayed for bad weather so they could catch up with their work.

Barrels of quahogs were shipped to New York, as many as fifty or sixty a day. In the Depression, the going price was $1 a bushel. Today it would be $31.15 a bushel. And during those years, littlenecks went for $1 a bushel as well, $0.50 for chowder clams. In 1966, littlenecks sold for $16 a bushel; today they would cost $157 a bushel.

Over in New Bedford, Campbell Soup Company bought as many as six hundred barrels of quahogs. That's a lot of clam chowder, no matter how you figure it.

Then there is lobster. Who knew the word *lobster* is derived from an Anglo-Saxon word for "spider"? Who knew lobsters could be right- or left-clawed?

The Martha's Vineyard Lobster Hatchery and Research Station was established near the Lagoon in 1951. Over decades, the late John Hughes and his associates oversaw the hatching of literally thousands of lobsters, which were then released into Island waters. We recognize Hughes's dedication and expertise in this unique operation.

Lobsters take about six years to mature and reach the legal one-pound size. They are protected by state and local regulations to maintain a stable, healthy population.

Eldridge's sold lobsters for $0.35 back in the day, but in 1966, they were going for $2.25 a pound. It's based on market price. "Everett Poole's grandfather used to say, 'when you make nothing, you can't save anything. If you make a lot, you can do without something, so you can save.'"[17]

This watercolor painting by Gilbert S. King depicts Poole's Fish House. It was a gift to Everett Poole by the artist's son, Tom King. It was painted on a Vineyard vacation in September 1960. Tom recalls the date, as he had just broken his right arm playing junior high football. *Courtesy of Tom King.*

Today, lobster sells for $16 a pound, in the shell, at Net Result. In 2023, a one-and-a-half-pound lobster sold for $24. Back in 1971, lobster meat was $9 a pound in a Menemsha fish market. Today, Net Result lists a pound of lobster, claw, and body meat at $75.

A lobster roll at Manning's Snack Bar in Gay Head was the epitome of summer delights. The business closed about 1970, much to Islanders' dismay.

In 1990, however, Grace Church in Vineyard Haven resurrected the delicacy. The church serves the ever-popular lobster rolls on Friday nights, all summer. Mary Tucker, wife of the bishop, initiated the popular lobster roll as a fundraiser for the church. And the American Legion also sells lobster rolls.

Codfish Soufflé

This sturdy-sounding dish was offered in the *Vineyard Gazette* in March 1910. Ironically, when the recipe was printed in the *Gazette*, "either cook or typesetter forgot to include the mortared and pressed fish in the final dish."

12 ounces cooked codfish
1 gill cream [a gill is ¼ pint or ½ cup]
2 tablespoons butter
½ teaspoon salt
2 tablespoons flour
Black pepper
1 gill fish stock
Nutmeg
3 eggs
Paprika

The fish must be rubbed through a sieve, then cooked over a low flame with the melted butter and flour. Once it becomes a smooth paste, beat in the eggs individually, add cream and seasoning; steam or bake 40 minutes.[18]

BAY SCALLOPS LIVE IN the ocean-fed ponds around Martha's Vineyard. Each of the six towns has a shellfish constable, even West Tisbury, with its access to the western side of Tisbury Great Pond. Town constables are tasked with the promotion of shellfish propagation through pollution control and predation or protection of the shellfish population. Aquaculture—the breeding, raising, and harvesting of shellfish—is a primary concern.

When a red flag flies by the bridges on State Beach, the shellfish beds are closed in Sengekontacket.

The public role of each town's shellfish constable is to oversee and enforce shellfish regulations in town waters, essentially ponds of ocean water.

Scalloping season depends on the location and type of scalloping but generally runs from October to March, a little longer for recreational scalloping than commercial.

Quahogs are accessible year-round, with a bushel a week the standard option. Everyone needs a license to gather shellfish, usually with a family permit. Check with individual town guidelines if you plan to go shellfishing.

A memorable highlight of family gatherings on the Vineyard was the old-fashioned clambake. First dig a huge hole in the beach sand and line it with stones. Light a fire and add hardwood so it burns an hour and a half. Rake off the embers and cover the stones with a thick layer of wet seaweed. Next, pile on the food: potatoes, chicken, corn, lobsters, and steamer clams. Cover it with seaweed and throw a canvas over it to keep the steam in. Raking sand onto the edges of the canvas seals the deal. Let it steam an hour, then serve.

We were ice skating on Crystal Lake in East Chop years ago when we noticed a peculiar sight: numerous large koi were captured in the ice. Most were frozen solid, but a few were moving their gills. It was memorable.

In the depths of the winter of 1778–79, after the British had devastated the Island economy by absconding with ten thousand sheep, Vineyarders were desperate for food. Someone noticed hundreds of striped bass, frozen solid in the northeast section of the Lagoon. "Word spread. Soon locals were breaking up the ice with pitchforks, shovels and whatever implements were available. Bass were piled up on the shore and divvied up among the townspeople to provide sustenance over the long winter ahead."[19]

Growing up, my mother ran the kitchen. One day when I was in high school, she had an appointment and put me in charge of the meal. She had made the tomato sauce for spaghetti, and as she was going out the door, she told me when to put the water on for the spaghetti and how long to cook it. I was half listening and mumbled, "OK."

At the appointed time I turned on the burner where she had left the large white enamel pot. After a few minutes, I checked, only to find the pot empty. I thought she had filled it with water. By now the pot was stuck to the burner!

Somehow, I managed to cook the spaghetti and the meal was saved, but my mother was not pleased with the white rings on the stove burner.

4
PORTUGUESE SPECIALTIES

Joyce and a college friend drove out to Menemsha for a picnic on the shore, sharing lobster rolls. The sharing got out of hand when a hungry seagull took a bite of her lobster roll, right out of her hand.

For a century and a half, whaleships sailed from Edgartown to capture whales for their blubber, boiled down to oil, used as a lighting source. When the electric light bulb came into use in 1879, whale oil was no longer in demand. By then, the whale population had been decimated in the Atlantic and the Pacific and was heading that way in the Arctic.

Setting off from Edgartown on their journey across the Atlantic, the whaling captain often left port without a full crew, sort of a shake-down cruise. The whaleship would stop in the Azores, one thousand miles off Portugal, or the Cape Verde Islands, four hundred miles off Africa. There they would sign up more crew, as well as replenish supplies of food and water.

The Portuguese of the Azores and Cape Verde were skilled sailors, coming of age on islands far out to sea. As hardworking crew on a years-long whaling voyage, many of these Portuguese seamen retired on Martha's Vineyard. Island life reminded them of home but with more opportunity. The sailors sent for their families and lived out their lives on the Vineyard, contributing to the Island lifestyle and sharing their favorite foods.

Two such settlements of Portuguese families evolved, one in Oak Bluffs on Vineyard Avenue and the other in Tisbury on Lagoon Pond Road. Both areas were known as Chicken Alley for the preponderance of chickens raised in those parts of town, used for eggs and meat.

Thus, the Mediterranean diet made its way to the Vineyard, transported by the Portuguese families. It has influenced and inflected the cuisine on Martha's Vineyard. Think linguica and chorizo sausage. Portuguese sweet bread, massa sovada, is mouthwatering. Parsley, mint, and coriander leaves are used in seasonings. Cornmeal is a staple of the Portuguese diet, as it is in both Native American and colonial fare.

One of the more popular Portuguese dishes is caldo verde, kale soup. A whole meal can be created around a hearty kale soup, featuring beef and beans, with a plate of fresh, hot cornbread; a fruit dessert; and a bottle of red wine.

Henry Beetle Hough celebrated Azorean or Portuguese cuisine, highlighting their Easter bread and linguica. Many recipes for delicious, wholesome meals migrated from the Azorean archipelago to find a place on the Vineyard dining table.

∽

Virginia "Ginny" Coutinho is a member of a third-generation Portuguese family. Her grandparents arrived on Martha's Vineyard from Madeira Island and the Azores. With them they brought many recipes that have endured and been sought after by family members and those wishing for an authentic Portuguese taste.

Ginny's grandfather Manuel "Manny" DeBettencourt was the founder of the Holy Ghost Feast, which continues to this day. Manny owned acres of land in the Wing Road area, and he staged the first Feast on his property. In the late 1930s, the Feast moved to the Portuguese American (PA) Club in Oak Bluffs, where it continues to be held. The Feast starts Saturday night as a social event.

Sunday morning begins with a parade from the steamship authority, up Circuit Avenue to the Catholic cemetery, then to the PA Club. A first communicant carries the crown, a symbol of thirteenth-century Queen Isabel, whose husband denied her the right to associate with the poor. She defied his wishes and would hide bread in the folds of her dress. One time the king questioned what was in her dress, and she replied, "Roses." When she spread her dress out, there was no bread but a bouquet of roses. She also allowed the poor and children to wear her crown, which influences the carrying of the crown to this day.

On Sunday of the Feast, a bowl of sopa or soupish (Espirito Santo Soup) is served to the attendees. Although many have thought the free soup was kale soup, it is not. The recipe for sopa contains cabbage, potatoes, beef, chourico, onions, and lots of fresh mint. Ginny's mother was known to say, "If you don't put the mint in, forget it!" The free sopa is a symbol of the generosity of Queen Isabel feeding the poor. Although Ginny's family routinely feasted on sopa or kale soup, her fisherman father would often bring home a stray lobster found in his fishing net.

Sweet bread was made at Easter. It was a long process with two risings, one overnight. Breads were often topped with a whole egg to represent rebirth or Easter resurrection.

When Joyce, a young bride, arrived on Island, a Portuguese woman gave her a loaf of sweet bread with three eggs on top at Easter. She said each egg represented a child. Without planning, Joyce eventually had three children.

Maca Sovada (Portuguese Sweet Bread)
By Alice Coutinho, Ginny's mother

5 pounds Pillsbury flour
1 ½ tablespoons salt
¼ teaspoon anise flavoring
1 can milk in quart bottle, remainder filled with hot water
4 cups sugar
12 eggs
2 yeast dissolved in ½ cup warm water
1 stick oleo or butter
1 large heaping serving spoon of Crisco

Mix liquids, beat in dry ingredients, let rise.

Cover with dish towel and warm blanket to keep out drafts. It is most satisfactory to make in early evening and let rise till double in bulk and push down before retiring.

Form into rolls and loaves in early morning and let rise till double in bulk and bake at 350 degrees 20 to 30 minutes, until golden brown.

Brush top with mixture of 2 egg whites and 3 teaspoons sugar, slightly beaten, and let stand in a tipped bowl while baking is going on. Use clear liquid only.

Topping
1 egg white
2 teaspoons sugar

Beat with fork until frothy, add 2 teaspoons sugar and mix. Put in small bowl. Tilt it so clear white goes down to bottom. Brush on bread before baking.

Soupish aka Sopa (Espirito Santo Soup) Served at the Feast
By Alice Coutinho

1 large onion, chopped
1 chourico sausage
1 shank bone with meat on it
1 green cabbage, cut in bite-size pieces
Whole potatoes, peeled
Salt and pepper to taste
Fresh mint
Loaf of Portuguese bread dried out so it is hard

Put meat in a kettle and cover with cold water. Add onion. Bring water to boil, skim off foam, then reduce heat and simmer gently until meat is almost done. Add 1 tablespoon salt (best to taste before adding more), dash of pepper and cook a little longer until the meat is tender.

Meanwhile, put chourico in another pan, cover with water, boil gently for about 15 minutes. Add whole potatoes, cabbage, and chourico to the soup. Cook until the potatoes are done.

To serve, break bread up into small pieces and put a layer of mint sprigs, then a layer of bread chunks in the bottom of the tureen. Keep making layers of bread, then mint, then bread, ending with mint on top. When soup is cooked and while very hot, pour on enough broth to soak through the bread. Cover tureen to keep hot. Serve soup in bowls, with meat, potatoes, and chourico on a separate platter.

Kerry Alley grew up on Vineyard Avenue, the Chicken Alley of Oak Bluffs. Three of his four great-grandparents came from the Azores and one from Ireland, which resulted in him being named Kerry. His great-grandfather Dominges Medeiros was a fishmonger who sold halibut. Because of his pronunciation, when he called out the word *halibut*, it began to sound more like *alley*. The name stuck, and in the 1940s, the Medeiros family name was legally changed to Alley.

Kerry recalls his mother making malasadas, fried dough. Saturday night she would make the dough and place it in a large pan covered with blankets. The warmth of the blankets caused the dough to rise, so by morning it was ready to be fried. Fried dough was a Sunday morning treat. As soon as word got out in the neighborhood that Betty Alley was making fried dough, family and neighbors descended on her house. When Betty could no longer manage the task, Kerry took over.

A specialty was pork, pickled in a brine overnight, then cooked. Of course, kale soup was a standby. Another favorite of Kerry's, when he was growing up, was grape nut pudding. However, marcela or blood sausage was not a favored taste. Kerry recalls his grandfather making wine with nearby grapes.

Another memory Kerry shared was of Joe Bernard's pigs. When a pig was about to be slaughtered, neighborhood children gathered round. One of the men would remove the pig's bladder, tie it up and give it to the kids to use as a ball. The first pigskin.

Kerry Alley is of Azorean descent. He grew up on Chicken Alley, aka Vineyard Avenue, Oak Bluffs. *Photo by Joyce Dresser.*

Black Dog Sauce

This chunky marinara works well with everything from eggs to pasta to meat. The Black Dog Summer on the Vineyard Cookbook offers ad lib freedom to the chef. This recipe should make six cups of sauce.

¼ cup olive oil
1 cup diced celery
1 cup diced onion
1 cup diced carrot
8–10 ripe plum tomatoes, coarsely chopped
1 (6-ounce) can tomato paste
½ cup red wine
5 cloves garlic, minced
3 tablespoons fresh oregano
3 tablespoons fresh basil
1 bay leaf
Salt and pepper

In a large saucepan, sauté the diced vegetables in olive oil until tender.

Add the coarsely chopped tomatoes. Add the tomato paste, wine, garlic, and herbs.

Simmer sauce 1 hour; check seasoning; add salt and pepper to taste.

Robin Rebello's parents were of Portuguese descent. To this day, Robin prepares the family's favorite, her turkey stuffing.

Robin's Portuguese Turkey Stuffing

1 package milk crackers, like Royal Lunch or Heritage crackers
Green pepper, onion, celery
Turkey gizzards
Linguica
Bacon
Bell seasoning

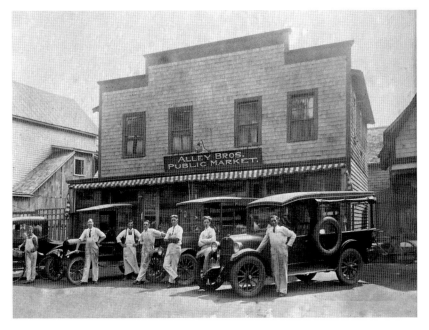

Kerry Alley's uncles ran Alley Brothers Market at Montgomery Square, off Circuit Avenue, in the early twentieth century. *Courtesy of Kerry Alley.*

Grind the milk crackers in a food processor or blender, leaving them in crumbs but not powdery.

Grind the remaining ingredients, then sauté them in lots of butter. Sprinkle with Bell seasoning.

Add just enough water to moisten the crackers.

Mix everything together and stuff the turkey.

Portuguese Kale Soup
From Alice Coutinho, Ginny's mother

1 pound kale
1 pound linguica, cut into ½-inch-thick slices
½ pound chourico, cut into ½-inch-thick slices
1 tablespoon olive oil
1 cup chopped onion

1 (13-ounce) can beef broth
½ teaspoon ground cumin
1 ½ teaspoons salt
1 clove garlic, minced
1 cup chopped green cabbage
2 quarts water
1 large or 2 medium Yukon Gold potatoes, peeled and diced (about 1 cup)
1 (16-ounce) can kidney beans with liquid

Rinse the kale well, then pick over and discard any tough stems and discolored spots. Cut the leaves crosswise into narrow strips and set aside.

Sauté the linguine and chourico in a stockpot over medium heat for 2 to 3 minutes, or until they have rendered some of their fat. Add the olive oil and onion and sauté for 3 minutes, or until the onion is translucent. Add the broth, cumin, salt, garlic, kale, cabbage, and water, raise the heat to medium-high, and bring to a boil. Lower the heat to a gentle simmer and cook for 1 hour, or until the kale and cabbage are very tender and the flavors have deepened and blended.

Add the potatoes and the kidney beans and their liquid and continue to cook for 15 minutes, or until the potatoes are fork tender. Remove from the heat, let cool, cover, and refrigerate overnight.

The next day, skim off the fat from the surface and reheat the soup. Ladle into bowls and serve.

The power failed during our dinner in a restaurant in St. John in the Virgin Islands. A waiter had to pry up a tile in the dining room floor to access the cistern to get water to wash the dishes. Staff handled the situation with a sense of calm urgency, as if they'd been there before.

5

AFRICAN AMERICAN SELECTIONS

As a little girl, Jo-Ann Walker accompanied her grandmother Sadie Ashburn to pick out a turkey for Shearer Cottage Sunday dinner. "They were so big," recalled Jo-Ann. "It's a wonder I can eat turkey today."

*D*r. Jessica Harris described the culinary influence of Thomas Jefferson. She credits him with incorporating African foods into the mainstream diet of the Virginia populace. He advocated for chefs and cooks, recognizing their talents and skills to put delicious foodstuffs on his table at Monticello.

It is common knowledge Jefferson had a liaison with his wife's half-sister, Sally Hemings, after his wife, Martha Skelton, passed in 1782. Sally Hemings bore him six children. Not as well known is that Sally's brother, James Hemings, also enslaved at Monticello, was Jefferson's cook. James Hemings learned hearth cooking, mastering spit jacks to roast meat and long-handled frying skillets, cooking food evenly on an open flame.

James Hemings was so renowned Jefferson had him sail across the Atlantic in 1784 to work alongside French chefs in Paris, where Jefferson served as a minister plenipotentiary, negotiating with the French in the postwar era. Sally Hemings was there as well. Later, Jefferson offered James Hemings the role of White House chef, but Hemings refused.

Dr. Harris recognizes "the culinary traditions of the enslaved, who brought their ways into the kitchen of the founding fathers and helped create such uniquely American dishes as catfish soup, peanut soup, and Virginia gumbo."[20]

Around 1900, the Black population increased on Martha's Vineyard. While not specifically tied to the Great Migration from the rural South to the urban North, many Blacks moved to Martha's Vineyard on a year-round basis in the early years of the twentieth century.

Two prominent Vineyarders inspired this population spurt. Jamaican minister Oscar Denniston led the Bradley Memorial Church to integrate Portuguese people into the Vineyard culture. And Blacks joined his church in great numbers. Former slave Charles Shearer and his wife, Henrietta, a free Black woman, opened Shearer Cottage in 1912, welcoming Blacks who were denied a room in white hotels.

Following the Second World War, Oak Bluffs became a popular Black resort, with people drawn by the Green Book to the welcoming Vineyard. The Highlands by Oak Bluffs Harbor and the Gold Coast, by Inkwell Beach, were popular enclaves for vacationing Blacks.

Many more Black tourists visited the Vineyard in the wake of President Barack Obama's Vineyard vacations and purchase of property on Island. Black retirees became year-round residents, appreciating the laid-back lifestyle and agreeable surroundings.

These varied waves of Blacks introduced special foods to the Vineyard; many have become standard American fare. Soul food dominates this cuisine.

Soul food originated in the South and moved north during the Great Migration, in the first third of the twentieth century, when six million Blacks relocated, seeking a respite from Jim Crow. Economic opportunity in industrial plants was preferable to working in cotton or tobacco fields in the Deep South, reminiscent of enslavement.

The term *soul food* originated in the 1960s in the Black Power movement. Soul food reflects the traditional cuisine of southern Blacks.

Soul food originated on the plantation. Ostensibly, the enslaved population was fed, clothed, and sheltered, but often they needed more food, which they planted and harvested for themselves. African American cuisine evolved by preparing enticing dishes with minimal ingredients. That cuisine reflects traditions and heritage of Black families.

Five staples make up prominent soul foods. Blacks recognize and honor these dishes, keeping them on the food chart of African American cuisine in the twenty-first century.

Collards are leafy greens often cooked with bacon, ham hocks, or smoked turkey. Seasoning with vinegar, salt, and red pepper flakes helps them partner with other soul food dishes.

Cornbread, made with cornmeal, flour, eggs, baking powder, and milk, can be cooked in a skillet, fried, or baked, then served with butter, honey, or molasses. Cornbread can become stuffing in a turkey or chicken; it is often shared with other soul food.

Fried chicken is a very popular soul food. To cook, bathe pieces of chicken with flour, spices, and buttermilk and then fry in oil until golden in color and crispy in texture. Fried chicken can be served with gravy or honey.

Macaroni and cheese is made with pasta, embraced by melted cheese, milk, butter, and seasonings. Chef Deon Thomas adds diced carrots, pepper, broccoli, and peas to liven it up. Bake until it bubbles and browns on top for a tasty crust. It goes well with many dishes.

Sweet potato pie is mashed sweet potatoes mixed with eggs, butter, spices, and often evaporated milk. Bake in a pie crust and top with whipped cream or marshmallow for a delightful dessert. Sweet potato pie is a traditional soul food, often served during the holidays.

Soul food has assumed a historic role in Black life. Soul food asserts Black identity, heritage, and family. And most important, soul food makes you feel good.

Shearer Cottage was the most prominent African American hotel on Martha's Vineyard. Period. The hotel opened in 1912. It became a haven for vacationing Blacks in The Highlands of Oak Bluffs for generations, popularized by the likes of Harry Burleigh and Adam Clayton Powell. New York Blacks followed them, vacationing on the Vineyard. And many settled on Island.

Jo-Ann Walker is a member of the Shearer family. She rhapsodized about the turkey dinner, with all the fixings, served every Sunday to Shearer guests. And while it was not a public restaurant per se, if someone sought to dine at Shearer, that could be arranged if there was room at the table.

Jo-Ann's grandmother Sadie Ashburn shopped for fresh fruit at the A&P, either in Vineyard Haven or Oak Bluffs, then returned to Shearer to bake her fruit pies, a favorite with Shearer guests.

Shearer Cottage, the first Black-owned hotel on Martha's Vineyard, welcomed vacationers and served delicious meals, especially on Sunday. *Photo by Joyce Dresser.*

As a teenager, Olive Tomlinson and four friends rode their bicycles out to Gay Head. Olive still recalls the experience, pedaling up those endless hills, seventy-plus years ago. The memory of the ride is still vivid, even if Olive doesn't remember whether their mission was a search for the best clam chowder or simply the adventure.

From the 1940s into the 1960s, Olive and/or her mother, known as Cutey, waited tables at Shearer Cottage. Olive confirmed Jo-Ann Walker's recollection of Sunday dinner as the height of hospitality. Turkey with gravy, potato, and vegetables, but not collards. And rolls. With fruit pie for dessert. Every Sunday. Thirty to fifty guests filled the dining room, enjoying the company and savoring the food.

Sadie Ashburn was known for her rolls. "She could make them with her eyes closed, walking backward," said Olive. "They were the best." Like Jo-Ann, Olive remembers going to the turkey farm with Aunt Sadie. Sadie would pluck and cook and serve the fowl to the delighted guests. It was an experience Jo-Ann and Olive remember fondly.

Breakfast at Shearer, said Olive, was "homemade New England baked beans, codfish cakes, and Sadie's homemade rolls. All homemade." She added, "We would request extra desserts and then hide them in the closets to eat later."[21]

We asked Olive about soul food, such as fried chicken, macaroni and cheese, and sweet potato pie. "I would kill for that," she said. Did she grow up on soul food? As a New Yorker, not a southerner, Olive's mother mastered "home cooking, which we loved; down home cooking, was the best."

Have you heard of the Rubber Dinner? Olive shares the tale.

During World War II, there was a rubber shortage; rubber was rationed, which limited driving. At the time, Olive's cousin Carol, also a little girl, got a doll made of rubber. That was a big deal. That doll was special. Carol loved her doll because it brought her attention.

One day her mother offered to make Carol a sandwich. Instead, Carol said she wanted a Rubber Dinner. She wanted a real dinner, not just a sandwich. Since that day, for Olive and her family and friends, and now you, dear reader, a Rubber Dinner means the real thing, home cooking, a down home meal. A Rubber Dinner is the best dinner, so special it makes your mouth water.

Martha's Vineyard does not have a soul food restaurant, but several Black chefs know how to put a delicious meal on the table.

Two Black chefs lead the way: Winston Christie runs Winston's Kitchen and Linda Jean's. Chef Deon Thomas runs the VFW. Both are at the top of their game. They offer Caribbean cuisine, as well as soul food and typical dishes.

A new face in town is Canieka Fleming of the Loud Kitchen at the Ritz Café in Oak Bluffs. Olive Tomlinson was impressed that Canieka worked with three Vineyard mentors: Gretchen Coleman, an African American; Juli Vanderhoop, a Wampanoag; and Jan Buhrman, a white woman. There's no one better to train you than this triad of superb chefs. "That's the Vineyard way," said Olive.

In her memoir *My Soul Looks Back*, Dr. Jessica Harris, a seasonal Oak Bluffs resident, recalls memorable meals with prominent African Americans. She addresses the menus of special meals, and the atmosphere, camaraderie, and recollections of these unique dining experiences.

Sharing Mediterranean soupe au pistou with James Baldwin stands out. Dr. Harris recalls the blue sky, "Jimmy's" welcome table, and the delightful feelings created in her head, her heart, and her taste buds. Food and friendship are memorable.

Summering in the Oak Bluffs cottage her parents purchased half a century ago, Dr. Harris noted, "Both the Island and I have changed a great deal in those years." She still celebrates Bastille Day with a leg of lamb, inviting old friends and new to her home.[22]

Ten Boy Curry was on the menu when Harris sat down with Maya Angelou in Sonoma Valley. Dr. Harris lists the ten "boys" in the curry dish: mango chutney, tomato chutney, chopped peanuts, raisins, finely grated coconut, lime pickle, fresh pineapple pieces, kachumber salad, raita, and papadum. Once again, it's the companionship, the atmosphere, and the memories that make the meal unique.[23]

After Chef Deon Thomas graduated from the Culinary Institute of America, he headed to Anguilla, where he eventually operated four restaurants. It was in one of his restaurants that Eleanor Pearlson met him and encouraged him to come to Martha's Vineyard. He arrived in 2000 and a year later opened the Cornerway in Chilmark. When the Cornerway closed for the winter, he returned to Anguilla.

After the Cornerway, he opened Deon's in West Tisbury and then moved to Oak Bluffs. He was still operating two restaurants in Anguilla, but in 2009, hurricanes ravaged them. In 2011, Chef Deon left Oak Bluffs and went to New York for a year. In 2012, he returned to the Vineyard with the intent to cater, finding a commercial kitchen at the VFW in Oak Bluffs. Beside the kitchen was a large room that has become his dining room.

His menu at the VFW consists of Caribbean and American fare. It includes favorites such as conch fritters, oxtail soup, Jamaican jerk chicken, barbecue spareribs, and buttermilk fried chicken, which these writers can attest is delicious. But the story doesn't end in the dining room.

Chef Deon is also a former pastor and now sees his ministry as preparing meals for the needy or those folks who can no longer manage a kitchen. In 2014, he began preparing weekly meals at the Methodist church and did so until neighbors in the Campground complained about the noise. Currently, he uses his kitchen at the VFW.

For the past thirteen years, he has prepared a weekly meal for the Island's community supper program. He also prepares up to five hundred Thanksgiving meals to go or dine in. In 2023, he roasted fifty turkeys, some from Arnie Fischer and North Tabor Farm. Much of the produce is donated by Island Grown Initiative and Morning Glory Farm. While some of the thirty volunteers, including his daughter, are peeling vegetables on Tuesday, Chef Deon brines the turkeys. On Wednesday the chopping begins, and he starts the stuffing.

The menu also includes a pumpkin ginger soup, potatoes, squash, collards, kale, and sweet potatoes.

Chef Deon Thomas is a pastor who uses his culinary talents to serve his parish, the community at large. *Photo by Joyce Dresser.*

Of course, there is dessert, often pies donated by Morning Glory Farm. Still recovering from long days and nights preparing for Thanksgiving, Chef Deon prepared Christmas dinner for three hundred people. In the dining room, some guests bring their own tablecloths and china to make it feel like home. The prevailing mood is happiness for the recipients, the volunteers, and especially Chef Deon.

Chef Deon is not alone in addressing food insecurity on the Vineyard. Meals on Wheels has been delivering hot meals to home-bound seniors since 1972 and currently has about 135 people on its daily delivery schedule.

"Meals are prepared one day in advance in the cafeteria of the Martha's Vineyard Hospital. Director of food and nutrition, Chris Porterfield works with elder services to create a monthly menu." This article in the *MV Times* sought volunteers to help with the deliveries.

Porterfield knows his clientele. In the past, he has worked with Island Grown Initiative to procure locally grown ingredients, such as purple potatoes. "We refuse to use the state's menu," he said. "We're serving people what they like.'"[24]

Seven churches serve meals: St. Andrews and Federated Church in Edgartown, First Congregational in West Tisbury, St. Augustine's, The Hebrew Center and Grace Episcopal Church in Vineyard Haven, and United Methodist Church in Oak Bluffs. Volunteers prepare the meals for seniors, shut-ins, or people in need of a meal. Originally, it was a social event, but since the pandemic, most meals are delivered to the house bound.

Harbor Homes feeds those in transitional housing, or homeless, on site in one of their two down-Island facilities. Hunger on an island of plenty may sound oxymoronic, but unfortunately, it is a reality.

In 1996, two of my three children were in college in Maine. We decided to celebrate Thanksgiving there. Of the five of us, Tom was a vegetarian and Christopher a vegan. I had two pots on the stove for gravy and mashed potatoes and stirred them simultaneously. Besides the free-range turkey in the oven, there was also Tofurkey. It was quite an operation, yet everyone was happy.

6

ETHNIC OPTIONS

Barbara Fenner's culinary skills contributed to Yankee *magazine awarding Menemsha Galley the Editor's Choice for Best of New England in casual dining in 2014.*

Joe Tomlinson, Olive's husband, was Jamaican. His mother always prepared a huge pot of beans and red peas with a pork base. Everyone agreed it was delicious. Olive fondly recalls her mother-in-law's pot of beans as mouthwatering. Olive's daughter-in-law is mainland Chinese. Olive represents the ethnic mix that is such a joy on Martha's Vineyard.

Immigrant groups are drawn to Martha's Vineyard, benefitting the Island with many wonderful dishes. From the migration of Portuguese meals via whaling ships to the soul food brought north with the African American population, the Vineyard welcomes meals from the people of Italy, England, Ireland, and Scotland. Asian restaurants—Japanese, Thai, Indian, and Chinese—have a foothold on Island. And more recently, the Vineyard has absorbed cuisine from Brazil and Jamaica.

Brazilians began to immigrate to the Island in the mid-1980s, and the population has blossomed in the twenty-first century. Brazilian food, religion, and soccer have made an impression with Islanders.

At the West Tisbury First Congregational Church, Marjorie Peirce oversees the preparation of weekly meals for Harbor Homes and community suppers. One week, she invited Brazilian Andrea Trindade to prepare a meal for Harbor Homes.

Andrea manned the stove with four dishes. Escondido, a favorite Brazilian dish, was first up. Although it is usually made with sausage, she opted to use ground chicken, which she sautéed in oil with onion, lemon juice, parsley, paprika, and Bodia, a seasoning with onions, garlic, salt, pepper, and various spices and herbs. Potatoes were boiled and then mashed with butter and milk. In a baking pan, Andrea spread some mashed potatoes, topped it with the chicken mixture, sprinkled shredded mozzarella cheese, then more potatoes and more cheese. It was baked until hot.

Another dish was beans. In a pressure cooker, Andrea covered dry brown beans with water. These cooked for fifteen minutes, and then she cooked them again with lots of sautéed garlic and added parsley. The beans accompanied the rice cooked with onions and garlic.

Finally, finely sliced cabbage, couve refogado or braised cabbage, was sautéed with onion in oil. Turmeric, salt, and pepper rounded out the dish.

The beans, rice, and cabbage were served side by side, while the escondido was presented in its pan.

Many young people from eastern Europe flock to Martha's Vineyard in the summer to work, driving a bus for the VTA, waiting tables at Linda Jean's, or housekeeping at the Pequot Hotel. Bulgarians, especially, say the "the food that tastes most like home" comes from the tiny takeout Caribbean Cuisine, next to Washashore Laundromat, in downtown Oak Bluffs.

Stacy and Newton Waite have run Vineyard Caribbean Cuisine since 2017. The Jamaican couple first opened their takeout at Five Corners in Vineyard Haven but have been in Oak Bluffs since 2019. The line of customers curls along Circuit Avenue Extension for chicken, beef, or veggie patties, fried rice, pasta salad, or oxtail, chicken dinners, and vegetarian options all summer long.

Prime dishes sell well. Ackee and saltfish is the national dish of Jamaica. Curry goat and jerk pork are popular. Other dishes invite the curious or satiate the native.

For the curious, ackee, the national fruit of Jamaica, grows year-round. Originally from West Africa, it flourishes in Jamaica. The fruit is ready

Right: As a minister, Andrea Trindade views her congregation as anyone she can help. *Photo by Joyce Dresser.*

Below: Andrea Trindade works with Marjorie Peirce to prepare a meal for Harbor Homes, which offers transitional housing and winter shelter on the Vineyard. *Photo by Joyce Dresser.*

Top: Carol Meikle prepared a Jamaican meal to share with her son Geovane's high school class. *Courtesy of Carol Meikle.*

Bottom: The Jamaican population on Martha's Vineyard has grown significantly, expanding Jamaican cuisine on the Island. *Courtesy of Carol Meikle.*

to pick when the red pods split and the fruit yawns or smiles. The fleshy sections, arils, hide beneath black seeds. Pick out the arils to cook and eat.

With many Caribbean consumers on Island, from year-round Jamaicans or visiting West Indians to the tourist off the boat, the menu of Caribbean Cuisine meets a diner's taste buds, schedule, and pocketbook. And while Chef Deon and Winston's also offer Jamaican dishes, Vineyard Caribbean Cuisine focuses solely on the authentic dish, without distractions of American food. It's takeout only, with a picnic table by the window.

Stacy and Newton Waite run Caribbean Cuisine, a summer business in downtown Oak Bluffs. *Photo by Thomas Dresser.*

Martha's Vineyard is a melting pot.

The Scottish Society of Martha's Vineyard, a small contingent of natives, descendants, friends, and families of Scottish people, has celebrated the birthday of Robert Burns (January 25, 1759) for more than three decades. Offering haggis pie, Stockman oatcakes, and Campbell's shortbread, with a nip of scotch, rekindles and honors traditions and memories of the Scottish diaspora.

For years, China House was the mainstay of "foreign" dining on the Vineyard. Located on Upper Main Street in Edgartown, China House is a full-service restaurant with wonton soup, egg rolls, and more. Net Result and the Lookout both serve sushi.

Copper Anchor, at the Mansion House, is a sushi bar and seafood restaurant. Mikado Asian Bistro offers Chinese and Japanese delicacies, including sushi, teriyaki, and sashimi. Mikado opened in Tisbury in 2017 and expanded to Oak Bluffs in 2023. The atmosphere is quiet and relaxing.

Oak Bluffs' Bangkok Cuisine is one of a chain of seven Thai restaurants based on the Cape. Its website notes, "Thai Cuisine offers some of the tastiest ingredients such as basil, ginger, coconut, and curry." It offers takeout or dine-in options. Thai dinners are a welcome alternative to Oak Bluffs' seafood and American cuisine.

Bombay Indian Restaurant serves authentic Indian food, in season. In 2022, Austin Grande, the owner, relocated the restaurant from the Martha's Vineyard Airport Business Park to Oak Bluffs, where it was voted best new restaurant on the Island.

$$\sim$$

Veggie haggis in Scotland. Seriously?

I walked along the West Highland Way with my daughter Jill in 2022. At the hostel in Inveroran, I ordered haggis, the national dish of Scotland. My veggie haggis was delicious but not cooked in a sheep's stomach, like the real thing.

7
SEASONAL TREATS

Vineyarders lock their cars only in zucchini season. No one wants a home gardener to leave a zucchini on your front seat. Enough already.

Martha's Vineyard offers a temperate climate and a unique growing season. With a coastal breeze and the Gulf Stream not far offshore, Islanders benefit from a cooler summer and a warmer winter. Farmers take full advantage of such opportunities; they plant and harvest the special treats visitors and locals anticipate throughout the growing season.

Salad Greens

Among the first plants to break ground in late spring are salad greens of various shapes and sizes, tastes, and textures. Greens are easy to grow and can be planted throughout the season, offering a steady supply of nutritious salad veggies, right in your garden.

Favorite greens include arugula, butterhead, kale, mizuna, and Romaine. Greens should be crisp, without wilting or yellowed leaves, the fresher the better. Salad greens improve a sandwich, a tortilla, or a side to egg salad or grilled chicken, the perfect add-on to a summer luncheon.

Morning Glory Farm is the go-to farm stand for premium vegetables, baked goods, and gourmet groceries. *Photo by Joyce Dresser.*

Pea Shoot, Pea, Watercress, and Arugula Salad[25]
Recipe by Robin Forte

¼ cup lemon juice
¼ teaspoon salt
Pinch black pepper
½ cup olive oil
4 ounces pea shoots
1 bunch watercress, stems removed
1 bunch arugula, stems removed
½ cup frozen green peas, thawed
1 tablespoon chopped mint
¾ cup crumbled feta cheese

In a small bowl, combine lemon juice, salt, and black pepper. Whisk in olive oil. Put washed, trimmed greens into a large bowl and toss with dressing. Top salad with green peas, chopped mint, and crumbled feta cheese.

Strawberries

On the Vineyard, the height of strawberry season is the summer solstice, but the berries ripen earlier with more sunshine, and the season is shorter if the spring brings lots of rain. They grow best in a raised bed.

Strawberries are in the family of roses, and their aroma confirms that definition.

Pink strawberries can be tart; crimson berries are overripe, tasting like wine. The best berries are bright red and sweet beyond belief.

Competition for strawberries comes from catbirds and wild turkeys, as well as homo sapiens, who love the delicious fruit. In June, the Harvest of the Month is strawberries, the perfect diploma for the Island Grown Schools Program.

Corn on the Cob

Vineyarders and visitors eagerly await the midpoint of summer for the first ears of corn. Few dining experiences top the typewriter dining style, turning the ear and mowing down one row after another.

Corn is the high point of the season, which can last six to eight weeks, if deer don't get them first.

Before we go from stalk to table, we must note the backstory of Morning Glory Farm, the largest farm by acreage and largest private employer on Martha's Vineyard. The original farm, a mere seventeen and a half acres, was picked up in auction eighty years ago by Debbie Athearn's father. He paid seven dollars for the acreage.

The first ears of corn Jim Athearn grew were not impressive. He sold them for a nickel an ear to an Edgartown market. Turns out the corn was full of worms. That was an inauspicious beginning for Athearn's farm stand, which opened in 1979. Today, Morning Glory is going strong and growing bigger and better, forty-five years later. Years ago, friends made corn a meal

Pumpkins offer a typical autumn scene on Island. Whether carving a jack-o-lantern or baking a pie, pumpkins are popular. *Photo by Joyce Dresser.*

in itself. They had a half-dozen ears, plenty of butter and salt, and a beverage of choice. What a delicious dinner.

Freshly picked corn is the top crop Vineyard visitors and locals alike recall with lip-smacking smiles. Whether steamed, boiled, or roasted in the husk on the grill, corn on the cob tops all seasonal Vineyard veggies.

One way we learned to cook corn was at the Square Rigger. Their corn was so sweet, we had to seek the technique. Boil the corn water with a half a cup of milk and a gob of butter for better taste.

Corn Chowder

The first chapter in *The Martha's Vineyard Cook Book* is titled "Chowders." The word derived from the French *chaudiere*, "iron pot." A chowder is a combination of seafood and milk boiled and served. Virtually any seafood may be used from clams to lobster, shrimp to fish, or even chicken and beef. Often potato or corn is added, along with bread, onions, and milk. "Tomatoes, however, used instead of milk in the chowders made further south, have always remained anathema in the chowders of New England."[26]

Carol Ward has a recipe for corn chowder:

Strip corn from its cob; sauté diced onion in butter, then add the corn kernels with enough liquid (made by boiling the stripped cobs in a veggie broth for about an hour) to cover. Simmer about 20 minutes. Remove about a quarter of the kernels from the pot. Set aside. Then blend remaining kernels in the pot to a smooth or nearly smooth consistency. Add milk, cream, or half-and-half to taste. Add the reserved kernels back into the pot. If you'd like a heartier chowder, now's the time to add some diced, boiled potatoes. Salt and pepper to taste.[27]

Beach Plums

The beach plum season is comparable to corn, ready to pluck in August through the end of September. Pollinated by wind or bees, beach plum fruit grows in summer, ready to be boiled into a delicious jam by Labor Day.

To make beach plum jam, pick a peck of ripe beach plums, which grow along the seashore. Ripe berries are the size of grapes. Wash and remove the stems; put in a pot with sugar and a little red wine for flavor. Boil until the skins start to split. Squeeze the plums through a food mill to remove stems and skin. Use the natural pectin of the beach plum to thicken the jam rather than adding pectin.

Replace the strained puree in the pot and let it simmer for nearly half an hour. The jam thickens as soon as it is removed from the pot. Fill sterile jars with the liquid, leaving a bit of space at the top. Put on the tops and boil for five minutes to get a decent seal.

That's all there is to it. The hardest part seems to be picking the berry itself![28]

Food is in abundance at the annual Agricultural Fair, from corn dogs to tempura and fried dough to strawberry shortcake. No one leaves the Fair with an empty stomach. *Photo by Joyce Dresser.*

Seasonal Fishing

Striped bass are the most popular gamefish off Martha's Vineyard. They arrive in late April or early May. The end of their season is autumn. Vineyarders are ready for stripers then.

The Martha's Vineyard Striped Bass and Bluefish Derby runs when the stripers are running, mid-September through October. Initially, a fishing derby was suggested to promote a new ferry line to the Vineyard in 1946. The Martha's Vineyard Rod and Gun Club agreed to sponsor the event, and it was a success from the start: one thousand fishermen, from twenty-nine states, converged on the Vineyard. It continues to draw enthusiastic anglers each fall.

Bluefish were added to the Derby a couple of years after it began. Bluefish. The most common fish in the sea. Fierce, voracious, prominent. And yet they tend to disappear, or so it seems.

In the pre-Revolutionary era, bluefish were everywhere. Fishermen assumed they were part of the environment, nothing special. Surplus blues were used to fertilize Island farmland.

And then it seems that in 1764, bluefish went below the surface; they didn't show their snouts in Vineyard waters. As Christine Schultz wrote, "Gone, every oily one."

It was more than half a century before they surfaced again, off southeastern New England. From the early 1800s to the end of the century, blues again ruled Vineyard waters, plentiful as ever.

Then it happened again. By 1891, there were no more blues. No blues until the 1930s, in the Depression, when food was scarce. Bluefish returned and have shared our waters for nearly a century.

It turns out environmental conditions affect fish, producing a deficit or a surplus. We're not suggesting climate change affected the bluefish population in the colonial era; perhaps the fish simply sought a varied diet. However, this historical measure gives us pause.

Bluefish revise their migratory patterns if the water temperature or currents change. Food sources affect their movement. Weather affects their locale, so they adapt, the senior blues as well as the young snappers. Today we recognize the threat of climate change, so let us celebrate the return of bluefish each spring.

"They're a great, great fish—tough, resilient, ferocious eaters," said Cooper Gilkes. "They bite off a lot of lures. It would hurt all of us in the tackle business if they disappeared."

To keep blues in Vineyard waters, we need a "buffer of biomass" or blues-in-waiting. Snappers must be "recruited" into adulthood. If they are dissuaded from hanging out in Vineyard waters, they might migrate to a more amenable environment. We don't want to lose our bluefish.

"On the Island, anglers watch for the first blue cutting up the flat water on the smooth side of a rip. The odds are the first one will hit a fisherman's lure sometime in the middle to end of May, when the lilacs and shadbush bloom."[29]

❧

"Martha's Vineyard has been a victim of the misguided notion that its cooks were chiefly inclined to the overcooking of vegetables, monotonous preparation of the stoutest foods, and a Puritanical avoidance of delicacy and imagination." Henry Beetle Hough worried people assumed Vineyard cooks did not know what they were doing.[30]

Hough insists that it is simply not true. The Island food favorites, detailed in Louise Tate King's *Martha's Vineyard Cook Book*, make the case categorically that the men and women of Martha's Vineyard are fully capable of preparing foods appropriately.

❧

We were friends with Roger, who lived up-Island and had access to many spots to pick blueberries. My former husband and he would spend a morning picking blueberries, so we had them stored everywhere and ate them daily. My children, aged about one and a half years and three and a half years old, delighted in blueberry pancakes almost daily. Their faces and clothes were smudged blue. I'm sure now those lands have huge houses on them and foraging for blueberries there is no longer an option.

8

FORAGING AND GLEANING

Each day, a Vineyard murder (flock of crows) flies across the Sound to forage on the Cape. In late afternoon, "the birds retreat to the Vineyard for rest, relaxation and refuge from their predators, primarily owls, which are more prevalent on the Cape than on the Island."[31] Talk about dining out!

*H*enry Beetle Hough recognized the benefits of foraging on the Island, from windfall apples and beach plums to cranberries and blueberries. Without hesitation, he advocated the Vineyard's culinary delights to be found in the woods, along the streams, and by the seashore.

Animals browse or graze for food, the very definition of foraging. It's what animals do, but it's also what humans are very capable of doing. Foraging is the search for and gathering of wild edibles, from fruits and berries to mushrooms and greens. Roots and nuts as well as seaweed are part of a forager's mission.

Native Americans see food as a connection to their family, their ancestral past. This link supports current dining habits and nurtures the health and happiness of the tribe. Heeding her elders, Juli Vanderhoop of Orange Peel Bakery recognizes the bounty around us, the nuts and berries, roots, and plants, that sustained her forebears and can help her today. Juli knows what is out there and harvests what she needs for her family. She recognizes the challenge to locate the right plants. Food from the ground, foraging, is not easy, but is there for those in the know.

Mermaid Farm is a self-service farm stand on Middle Road for customers who know what they want. *Photo by Joyce Dresser.*

For those without a heritage of Native traditions, Linsey Lee's book *Edible Wild Plants of Martha's Vineyard* is a primer for local foragers. From milkweed to sumac, beach rose to pokeweed, the berries, roots, and fruits of native plants await. As Lee wrote, "The early settlers realized that they too must live in close harmony with nature if they were to survive on this isolated island.…The Islanders learned to live in a state of almost total self-reliance."[32]

The benefits of foraging are numerous. First, it's free. If you go with someone knowledgeable in foraging, you'll discover fresh and nutritious delights hidden in plain sight. Your immune system will benefit if you harvest plants with vitamins, minerals, or antioxidants useful in avoiding chronic diseases.

It's rewarding to walk through the undergrowth and forage for blueberries or blackberries off bushes by the side of the path. Or beach plums along the shore. And there's nothing wrong with a little physical activity and mental health, living off the land, even for a short time. Although you need a license, foraging for shellfish—like scallops, mussels, or clams—is a great activity, as well as a source of nutrition.

With more than one hundred conservation sites on Martha's Vineyard, there is plenty of wooded land to meander through, searching for plants and berries, nuts, and roots. Sheriff's Meadow invites foragers to visit Huckleberry Barrens Preserve in Katama, specifically to forage.

Private land should be avoided, because, simply put, that's trespassing. With plenty of public property along the seashore, ponds, and streams and in the 5,600-acre State Forest, a lot of foraging is available, if you know where to look.

Foraging is accessible for those who seek. Or you can just pull into Cronig's or Stop & Shop and fill up your shopping cart.

Community Supported Agriculture links a farmer's produce to consumers, eliminating the middleman. Pay a given amount in the spring and receive a bounty of veggies throughout the growing season.

In the early 2000s, we joined a Community Supported Agriculture program at Whippoorwill Farm, site of the IGI Hub today.

What could go wrong?

First, I wrote, "They lure you in with a few tasty veggies early in the season, and before you know it, you're inundated with a flood of carrots and onions, turnips and beans, potatoes, and squash. Then a wayward radish lands in your lap."

That was a facetious retort to the fruits of the harvest. Yet it was very real.

We drifted through early summer with savory peas, fresh greens, and ripe strawberries. "Yet as Labor Day approaches, be on guard for an onslaught, a deluge of delight that overwhelms right on through to Thanksgiving—and this past year, even to midwinter."

Through the fall, "My wife and I struggle to close the refrigerator door as cauliflower and cabbage block access, peppers and tomatoes back up, and the fresh veggie drawer is jammed."

We tried to handle the onslaught. We bought a second refrigerator. Now we had plenty of room, except, "a fridge doesn't wash, cut, sort, bag, or store the veggies, never mind cook them." When we opened the refrigerator door, we were startled to see the veggies, "staring out accusingly when we glance inside."

A full refrigerator overwhelms us. We use the latest corn or tomato; leeks and bok choy get stuffed in back, untouched by human hands.

And we were not alone. Fellow CSA recipients were also drowning in the bounty. We shared recipes as we commiserated with those who could not keep up.

Facetiously, I suggested inventing a Rube Goldberg machine to wash, chop, bag, freeze, sort, and then cook our cornucopia, but that omitted the eating part. Must we dine a dozen times a day, in season?

We had to accept responsibility and "sincerely and religiously pick up our weekly produce, return home and calmly process the veggies."[33]

The next year, we replaced the CSA in favor of gleaning. The surfeit of veggies still has not been solved.

In 2020, the Department of Agriculture surveyed the national population. Results indicated 10 percent of all households did not have sufficient food. The study confirmed people of color have a high rate of poverty and food insecurity, especially during periods of economic uncertainty.

In 2023, Island Grown Initiative had 4,200 people registered with the Island Food Pantry. That means 20 percent of the year-round population live with food insecurity. (It should be noted, those people visiting the Food Pantry include summer residents, when the overall population is much, much greater.)

Gleaners gather hundreds of pounds of winter squash at a Morning Glory field, under the auspices of Island Grown Initiative. *Photo by Thomas Dresser.*

The National Gleaning Project, developed at the Vermont Law and Graduate School, combats food insecurity. Food recovery and the means to feed the hungry are essential to the safety net in this country. On the Vineyard, we like to think that food insecurity does not exist. It does.

The Pork to Fork program on Martha's Vineyard exemplifies a can-do creative program to deal with food waste. Since 2019, Jo Douglas has driven around the Island to pick up food remains and scraps from a couple of dozen restaurants. She feeds tidbits and leftovers to her pigs. When the pigs are ready for slaughter, the pork is resold to the restaurants. (Thomas Humphrey of the *Vineyard Gazette* noted, "Last year, she added a Leaf to Beef cow pasturing operation to the mix, another summertime operation.")[34]

Gleaning refers to gathering crops left on farmers' fields after the harvest. Gleaning provides nutritious harvested food to those in need.

In the Bible's Book of Ruth, the widow Ruth gleans the harvest, providing food for herself and her mother-in-law, Naomi, also a widow.

As the barley harvest begins, Ruth and Naomi return to Bethlehem. Ruth ventures out to glean. Boaz owns the field; he had heard of Ruth caring for Naomi. Boaz responds kindly to Ruth and encourages her to keep gleaning through the barley and wheat harvests.

In biblical times, gleaning was mandated to provide sustenance for the poor. In Deuteronomy and Leviticus, farmers leave the edges of fields unharvested for the poor to glean surplus crops. Grapes in the vineyards and olives on the trees are left for the needy.

The poor, the transient, those in need should be permitted to take what they can find in the fields, after the farmers have taken their harvest. Gleaning has biblical origins.

In the Middle Ages, the poor were permitted to wander the fields of the castle after crops were harvested. Squash, tubers, and beans were left. Peasants anticipated the glean; it was their food security.

"So there I was," Tom wrote in the *Vineyard Gazette* in August 2011, "hurtling along the Edgartown–West Tisbury Road in my 1948 red Willys Jeepster convertible, the wind blowing my hair, sun shining on my face, and 200 pounds of patty-pan squash riding comfortably with me in my open air vehicle. Was this a dream? Had I robbed a farm stand or was I planning to feed famished friends?"

Just a few days prior, Noli Taylor spoke about the Island Grown Initiative to "connect farmers with Islanders, through the schools, through beekeeping, through a Vineyard slaughterhouse project, a poultry project, and gleaning."

"Gleaning? Isn't that some fourteenth-century program where serfs pick through the fields of the manors to find a bit of sustenance, a leftover turnip or forgotten grains? Right! And we have gleaners on the Vineyard in 2011? Right again!"

I found myself "with a dozen compatriots in the back forty of Morning Glory Farm in Edgartown. Our assignment, as explained by Jamie [O'Gorman, of IGI], was to harvest the patty-pan and zucchini squash from several rows. Morning Glory had picked all they could sell at their stand.

"At first I felt like a migrant worker or feudal serf, but the experience grew on me, as I picked pound after pound of fresh yellow squash, and carted box after box off the field." The story continues. "In a little over an hour we harvested more than 600 pounds of squash; another contingent brought in 145 pounds of lettuce. (FYI: bags of lettuce are lighter than boxes of squash, so if you have back issues, I'd head for the lettuce.)"

Later, "Jim Athearn, proprietor of Morning Glory, strode by to see the fruits of our labors." He appreciates the volunteers with IGI. "'And I'm impressed at all you volunteers, willing to do the work,' he said with a smile."

That piece stands the test of time, especially the last paragraph: "The day's harvest exemplified living locally, helping feed those in need, and taking advantage of volunteers or interns to accomplish a worthy goal. It was a rewarding experience: fun in the sun and we got the job done."

Gleaners earn compensation. Volunteers are rewarded by taking some of the crop. Whether it's salad greens, tomatoes, corn, or potatoes, gleaners harvest the crops and then enjoy the bounty themselves. It's a win-win program.

Island Grown Initiative organizes each glean, assigning volunteers to glean the vegetables farmers do not need. On occasion, farmers plant crops simply to be gleaned.

Vegetables from Vineyard soil are weighed, sorted, and delivered to groups in need: senior housing, senior centers, the Food Pantry, the schools, the Native Americans, and even the Dukes County House of Correction. Everyone appreciates this bounty.

"The 200 pounds I transported to the Oak Bluffs School was processed the next day into 27 gallons of squash. I don't want to hear that Oak Bluffs students don't like squash."

Tom's college friend John and Leah, his partner, visit annually and treat us to dinner. In 2023, they chose l'etoile, where we enjoyed a scrumptious meal. Our waitress, Ariana, shared her story.

A Waitress Who Doubles as a Dietitian

My name is Ariana. I am a twenty-eight-year-old registered dietitian. I had the pleasure of meeting Tom and Joyce Dresser when they dined at l'etoile. So yes, I am also a server!

To tell my story, let's rewind a decade or so ago.

My love for the Island reverts to my childhood. Growing up in central Massachusetts, it's a quick drive plus a ferry to Oak Bluffs. My parents, brother, and I would stay at the Attleboro House, on Oak Bluffs Harbor. I have memories walking up and down Circuit Avenue, biking to the beach, and taking pictures of the gingerbread houses. The Vineyard has always been one of my favorite places.

Fast-forward to my early twenties. I began a master's program to be a registered dietitian. I have a passion for wellness. Many chronic diseases are manageable, based on the foods we eat and our lifestyles. I want to help others become the healthiest versions of themselves.

Registered dietitian candidates are matched to a program and undergo 1,200 hours of supervised practice, then sit for boards.

I promised if I got a match, I would reward myself by spending the summer on Martha's Vineyard. I wanted independence before venturing into adulthood. I got a match to the University of Saint Joseph. I would move to the Island.

Island life for seasonal workers is not that glamorous. Those beautiful mansions in Edgartown are summer homes. I considered living in one as a family's "summer girl," until I learned I would not have any days off.

I got a job as a server at the Atlantic, my first serving gig after working in food service in other capacities: a nutrition assistant, diet aide, diet clerk, dishwasher.

And so, it began—my first summer "on Island."

It was a good one, filled with countless doubles at work, beach trips, bonfires, new friendships, heartbreak, a summer fling, money saved; everything I had hoped it would be.

The Island has a way of calling you back. I worked at l'etoile that second summer, and it was better than the first. I passed my RD exam and got my dream job at Massachusetts General Hospital as a medical/surgical weight loss dietitian.

I moved to Boston. It's 2020 now. The pandemic hit, so back to the Island I went.

Living on the Island gave me perspective. I make connections that feel aligned. I breathe differently here. This Island has seen me through some of my highest highs and lowest lows.

I asked Martha where I should go. A woman walked by in a shirt that said aloha. A stranger on Lucy Vincent Beach told me about his trip to the Hawaiian Islands. Many synchronicities. I felt I needed a change.

In 2022, I moved to Oahu, Hawaii, with my dog. I worked as an RD at a nursing home and bartended at a pub. I learned to surf. I organized farm-to-table events and taught kids how to plant sunflowers. I spent most of my days at the beach. That year taught me more lessons.

It was time to leave, but I wasn't ready to come back to the New England cold after a year in Hawaii. So, I went through Dietitians on Demand for a travel contract at a hospital in Florida and spent a winter there. But I missed the Island. I served at l'etoile again, also working at a nursing home and hospital on the Cape.

My career path has not been conventional, but I wouldn't change a thing. My goal was to continue to travel, while working with more security than contract jobs.

Yes, I will be back to the Island next summer, working a few shifts at l'etoile. I'm not sure what this winter has in store yet, but I'll be booking some flights!

Ariana!

On a trip to Paris in 2012, we planned to meet up with my brother Richard and his wife at the apartment we had. After a bottle (or two) of wine, we wanted to go out to dinner. The only restaurant we knew was about three blocks away. Off we went. Sitting in a crowded room, my sister-in-law looked up to see a familiar face. "That's Caleb," she said. Caleb is my brother George's son. Yes, unbeknownst to us, he was in Paris at the same time as us, in the same restaurant, dining in the same room. What are the chances? [A quick glance at the yellow pages indicated some six thousand restaurants in Paris!]

9

THE FARMERS MARKET

Students from the West Tisbury school encouraged voters to ban plastic straws. The next year's class followed suit, banning plastic bottles across the Island. Way to go, WT.

A farmers market was organized on Martha's Vineyard in 1934 to provide fresh local food at lower prices than markets. Residents were suffering through the Depression. Lower prices were greatly appreciated.

The Market was founded by four women: Mrs. Argie Humphrey, Mrs. Orland Davis, Mrs. Daniel Manter, and Miss Hilda Austin. The Market ran twice a week at the Grange Hall, then known as Agricultural Hall. As many as twenty-two vendors sold their wares, which ranged from baked goods and chowder to seasonal vegetables.

At the opening Market of the 1936 season, nine people set their booths in "a wholesome and decorative appearance," according to the *Vineyard Gazette*. Crepe paper added a decorative flair to a couple of booths.

The newspaper noted a lack of rain slowed maturation of many vegetables, although there were still plenty of beets, spinach, lettuce, and peas. Shelves laden with homemade cakes, cookies, jams, jellies, "and many another toothsome goody were hunger-provoking indeed." And "a plenteous supply" of canned seafood and dozens of fresh eggs added to the sale items.

Customers meandered through Agricultural Hall all day long. Most vendors considered the opening of the Market a "gratifying success."[35]

Five years later, in 1941, the onset of World War II forced the Farmers Market to shut down, due to gas and sugar rationing. Argie Humphrey oversaw the Market at the time, and the closure precipitated a new career for him as a baker. Humphrey and his wife, Bernice, opened the Vineyard Foodshop in Vineyard Haven and later built a new bakery by their house in North Tisbury, across from the lone oak.

Today, Life at Humphrey's is alive at the Woodland Center off State Road. It is run by our son-in-law Pete Smyth, former owner of Slice of Life in Oak Bluffs, and Donna Kirby Diaz, granddaughter of Argie. Life goes on.

The *Vineyard Gazette* noted the gap between the closing of the Farmers Market in 1941 and its revival in 1974. "At some point it went fallow but thanks to hippies and retired English teachers, always a potent combination, it was revived in 1974 and has flourished ever since."[36]

During another economic downturn, the Farmers Market was successfully rejuvenated as a veritable feast of produce: "Vegetables, just picked from the garden, can be as colorful and as totally seductive to the eye as a bouquet of flowers, and bring joy to the palate as well." That heraldic welcoming by the *Vineyard Gazette* marked the rebirth of the Market in July 1974.

Options were many. Ranging from carrots and peas to beets and beans, fresh vegetables again filled booths at Agricultural Hall. Dozens of eggs, luscious loaves of home-baked breads, and juicy preserves set the market on a path to promote local produce.

Susan Whiting deserves credit for the revival of the Farmers Market. She recognized that high prices of fresh produce were prohibitive for many Islanders. By eliminating the middleman, she gave Vineyarders a break. Home gardens often produce more produce than the gardener can use. The Farmers Market distributes surplus vegetables. As a forerunner to Island Grown Initiative, the Market redistributed local food where most needed.

Whiting invited fifty people as vendors, promoting Island products. Each vendor paid a dollar a day and was responsible for their stand and cleanup. Fresh produce deserves a fair price, as it is locally grown and transported from garden to market to table.

The Vineyard Conservation Society promoted the Market, which succeeded with sufficient community participation.[37]

The Farmers Market draws locals and tourists to its Saturday and Wednesday offerings from early summer through late autumn. *Photo by Joyce Dresser.*

Charlie and Teena Parton were longtime vendors at the Farmers Market. Teena shared her recollections.[38] "Good memories of the WT Farmers Market!" She recalled, "It must have been in the early '90s. The market was held at the old Grange Hall on Saturday mornings and Wednesday afternoons. There were up to forty vendors, making it the largest in the state at that time."

Teena continued, "The Town required us to hire a policeman to control road traffic and a parking lot with attendants. We found it important to enforce a gate opening time by ringing a bell, since many would come early and clean out special items.

"It was necessary to put Khen Tran's spring roll stand near the parking lot end of the market, else the line of eager customers would block other booths! Unfortunately, the town board of health would not allow a seafood truck at that time. Vendors were required to be set up before opening and stay until closing, even if sold out. Wednesday afternoons were smaller and quieter than Saturday mornings."

Teena recommended Ethel Sherman's book, *The West Tisbury Farmers Market: Behind the Scenes*. She concludes, "Many good memories!"

Over the years, many Vineyarders have assumed the role of manager of the market initially run by Argie Humphrey in the 1930s and reborn in the 1970s under Susan Whiting. Prudy Whiting ran the market before Lois and Bob Daniels in the early 1980s. From 1986 to 1997, BZ Riger-Hall and Robin Fitzpatrick were in charge. At the end of the 1990s, Teena Parton and Jack Reed took their turn. From 2000 to 2006, Andrea Rogers and Prudy Burt ran the show. Debbie Koines served a stint as manager, and the basic format of the market continues. Going forward, Ethan Buchanan Valenti runs the West Tisbury Farmers Market as of this writing.

On June 10, 2023, the Farmers Market opened its fifty-sixth season at the new Agricultural Hall on Pan Handle Road in West Tisbury with these

Matt Dix of North Tabor Farm is a fixture at the Market, happily selling his produce to one and all. *Photo by Joyce Dresser.*

welcoming words: "The market offers free parking and admission, but dogs and cigarettes are not allowed."

Once more the Farmers Market drew summer crowds eager to partake in the preponderance of produce, fresh and seasonal, sourced in Vineyard farms. Flowers and sea salt, chocolates and goat milk soap added to the range of product at the Market. From egg rolls to alpaca yarn, there was no shortage of variety. The Market has proven its attraction each Saturday and Wednesday from nine o'clock to noon, a certified and enduring success.

When you return with a bounty of fresh vegetables, the next project is what to do with your winnings. Susie Middleton of *Martha's Vineyard Magazine* offers the succulent suggestion of a harvest salad. She provides easy-to-follow directions for assembling a party salad with grilled or roasted vegetables sufficient to feed a good-sized crowd. It's different and can be varied to meet individual wants and needs. As Susie said, "Your vegetables will thank you."[39]

Susie's recipe includes slicing squash and eggplant, brushing with oil, then grilling. She combines fresh chopped herbs like parsley, mint, basil, and cilantro with grains. Then she mixes sundried tomatoes, olives, and garlic with a bit of salt and vinegar, adding wheatberries, fresh tomatoes, cucumbers, and leaves of lettuce. Create your own concoction. The variety makes a delicious harvest salad with local produce.

Whether you're a tourist, a summer person, or a local, put the Farmers Market on your itinerary.

And the Farmers Market doesn't end on Labor Day. It continues into the autumn. Late in the fall, the Market relocates inside the Ag Hall itself, so there is warmth and camaraderie in the old barn, reconfigured from a New Hampshire farmstead in 1995, still meeting community needs.

On our first wedding anniversary, our friends, Judy and Peter Williamson and Joyce and John Balboni, invited us to the beach for a sunset supper. On the beach they had arranged a dining table and chairs, complete with tablecloth, flowers, and beautiful place settings. They pulled out a salad and pasta with alfredo sauce that had been wrapped in coolers. It was a delicious, delightful, and memorable meal.

10

REMEMBER?

Actor Jimmy Cagney, in California, called the state police on Martha's Vineyard. He requested Sergeant Altieri send him native scallops and quahogs. The officer complied. It was 1940.

Mollie Doyle recalled, "When I was a child, my '70s Martha's Vineyard food experience was essentially grilled Cracker Barrel Cheddar cheese sandwiches on Pepperidge Farm white bread, clingy clam chowder from any of the Island food shops, an occasional muffin from the Black Dog, and a boiled lobster at the Home Port for an adult's birthday."

Doyle shared more of her dietary memoir: "I think we went to Le Grenier and the Kelley House for a meal once or twice, and maybe Helios too. Then restaurants began popping up. The Oyster Bar, Feasts, and the Roadhouse come to mind. With them came a new kind of food culture, where Island-grown food and seafood began to be embraced and celebrated."[40]

With Mollie's memories as an appetizer, we share a few comments on myriad restaurants that once brightened the culinary landscape of Martha's Vineyard. We savor recollections of their potent tastes and treats, quirky idiosyncrasies, and tangible experiences, of what once was, but is no more.

THIS IS A PARTIAL list of bygone establishments; our apologies for omitting some favorites.

A poster of a hot dog and a Coke for fifteen cents reminds us of a bygone era. *Courtesy of Benito's Hair Styling.*

A&W

The A&W was at Five Corners in Vineyard Haven, adjacent to Stop & Shop. You could walk right in off the street, as it had no walls. A&W was a favorite hangout with big barrels of root beer, right there. Floats, burgers, and fries supplemented the root beer, always on tap.

Anthony's Restaurant

From 1979 to 1988, one of the more popular Island establishments was Anthony's Restaurant on Seaview Avenue in Oak Bluffs. Prior to Anthony's, the building had been the clubhouse for the golf course of the Island Country Club. When the club went bankrupt, Anthony "Tubby" Rebello was able to procure the clubhouse. After spending a year remodeling the building, Anthony's opened in 1979.

Anthony's was a year-round restaurant run by Tubby; his wife Marilyn; daughter Robin; and sons Todd and Christopher. The restaurant was open seven days a week and closed only for a few weeks for maintenance. Tubby took care of the back of the house while Marilyn ran the dining room and functions. Todd and Christopher tended bar and worked in the kitchen. Robin waitressed. Todd's wife, Mia, and Christopher's wife, Lynn, joined the staff as waitresses. Tubby's mother, Adeline, also worked, manning the register seven days a week. Members of the family were always present to greet their guests. The dining room seated 160 people, the bar had 9 seats, and the lounge could hold 50 people.

The menu had dishes to delight every customer, with a range of baby rack of lamb, veal piccata,

Anthony "Tubby" Rebello ran Anthony's Restaurant in the 1980s. His son Todd keeps the memories alive. *Photo by Joyce Dresser.*

prime rib, shrimp scampi, and Island Bay scallops. The shrimp scampi had large, butterflied shrimp, dipped in egg, dusted in flour, then quickly cooked in butter, with garlic and white wine. The shrimp were popped in the oven for a few minutes and served with rice on the side.

Homemade dinner rolls were a treat, and when homemade pecan rolls were introduced, customers came in just to buy them.

From 1979 to 1984, the restaurant added a salad bar. This was not your standard salad bar, but offered forty-five items, including mussels and clams on the half shell. Customers could choose the salad bar as their meal or have it with their entrée. The dessert menu was extensive, with cheesecake, crème de menthe parfait, strawberry pie, pecan pie, grape nut custard, bread pudding, and stellar ice cream puffs with hot fudge or butterscotch sauce on the side.

Robin recalls her favorite dish was Tornados and Crab. This was a filet mignon cut through the middle, then pan seared. On the plate, it was covered with Bordelaise sauce, Alaskan King crab meat, and then Bearnaise sauce.

One reason Anthony's was so successful was the consistency of the meals. Diners could count on their favorite dishes always being prepared the same way. Over the years, several chefs manned the kitchen: Roy Martel, David Norton, John Goldthwait, and Dennis Marshall.

On Saturday, there was often music in the lounge. Popular bands included Dick Aranjo, who played country western music; Taylor Made (Buck Taylor and his brother); Gene Baer and Ed Larkosh; and Spoof, whose members included Troy Tyson, Merrily Fenner, Betsy Medowski Gately, David Wilson, and Nathan Siktberg. The lounge was usually filled with dancers and onlookers.

New Year's Eve was a fun time at Anthony's with a band and good food. Anthony's served Thanksgiving dinners all day, and the family enjoyed theirs around nine o'clock that night. The venue was perfect for weddings, and many, many receptions were held there. At that time, receptions were held in the early afternoon, so as soon as the wedding party left, the restaurant was cleaned and ready for the evening diners. Donna and Jaime Leon enjoyed their wedding reception at Anthony's.

Todd Rebello recalls his favorite memories were weddings, as everyone was so appreciative. On Saturdays, after a wedding and evening diners, the family would sit around in the late evening and share their day.

Robin remembers a day she was to waitress for a luncheon. Neither the bartender nor the dishwasher came to work, so after Robin took drink orders, she ran to the bar to make the drinks, then serve them. When the luncheon was over, she became the dishwasher.

Another memory was the evening she was serving six people. One gentleman was particularly ornery and at one point shook his finger at her, saying, "I'm going to get your job! I know the owner." In a deadpan response, Robin replied, "Oh, you know my father?" The gentleman looked abashed, was very pleasant the rest of the night, and left a nice tip.

In 1988, Tubby and Marilyn were ready to retire. Family members were ready to try new endeavors, and so the business was sold to a Mr. Hayes. He renovated the building and was in business for two years before going bankrupt. In 1991, Paul and Kathy Domitrovich bought it, opened it as Lola's, and ran it for many years.

Fond memories of Anthony's linger with local customers. The family enjoyed the business. Prominent customers, like Michael Dukakis, Walter Cronkite, Jimmy Cagney, and Beverly Sills, often dined at Anthony's. It was a key part of the Vineyard dining scene.

When Robin's son Jared turned nine, he told his mother he wanted to bring a friend to dinner at Anthony's. Joyce's daughter Jennifer accepted his invitation. Robin and Jared came to pick up Jennifer. Jared came to the house to get her, opened the car door, and got in beside her. Before entering the restaurant, he told his mother she had to sit at the bar because he didn't want her near them. Jared's grandmother Marilyn, who was hosting, brought them to a table, and Bernadette was their waitress.

Both Jared and Jennifer ordered a chicken dish. Bernadette noticed Jared wasn't eating his chicken and asked him if he would like her to cut it up for him. He replied, "Yes please." Neither wanted dessert, and Jared paid the bill. On the way home, he said to his mother, "Bernadette tried to get us to buy dessert! She just wanted more of my money!"

The Bite

The Bite was a delightful little shack in Menemsha with a great following. The staff was always friendly, and the food was always delicious. Tom recalls one of the students who rode his school bus, Mary Morgan, worked there at a young age. It was always a treat to see her. Mimi Torchin felt "the crushing loss of the Bite in Menemsha. No fried seafood can ever compare nor the thrill and anticipation of the first visit of the summer.

There are no fried clams anywhere to compare and I loved their fried oysters." And yet, The Bite is no more.

Bittersweet

Located next to Middletown Nursery in the late 1990s, Bittersweet was on the site once held by Wayside, the Roadhouse, later by Icehouse, and now reconfigured as State Road, the premier up-Island restaurant.

Blueberry Hill

Lewis King married Louise Tate in 1939, and a decade later they moved to Martha's Vineyard. In 1951, they purchased 120 acres in Chilmark and built an inn on the property and a house for Lew King's parents. Blueberry Hill was on North Road near the Native Earth Teaching Farm.

Blueberry Hill Farm opened in 1952, serving breakfast, lunch, and dinner for its guests. Louise Tate King was already a skilled chef, so she stepped in to prepare gourmet dinners. This experience served her well in coauthoring *The Martha's Vineyard Cook Book* in 1971. Meals were served family-style on a long table in the farmhouse. Lewis King was the host, pouring wine and hobnobbing with the clientele.

The Kings divorced in 1961. Louise Tate King opened a seasonal French restaurant at her home in North Tisbury and another dining establishment in Edgartown.

Lew King remained at Blueberry Hill, offering special dinners such as French Mediterranean fish soup and Island bay scallops. He purchased seafood from Poole's Fish Market in Menemsha. One of his idiosyncrasies was to demand the bones remain on the mackerel, flounder, bluefish, and scup in his bouillabaisse. He claimed that gave his soup its unique flavor.

King sold Blueberry Hill in 1994. The restaurant continued operations until the economic downturn forced its closure in 2008.

Boston House

Krikor Barmakian renovated an old hotel on Circuit Avenue, the Cottage City House, into an ice cream parlor and café about 1916. He named it the Boston House, serving American and Chinese cuisine, and ran it for thirty years, according to Chris Baer's This Was Then column in the *MV Times*.

George Munro bought the restaurant in 1946, rebranding it as Munro's Boston House. It changed hands in the 1980s, converted into the Atlantic Connection and Seasons Restaurant. The AC was a venue for parties and concerts such as Ben E. King or a zydeco band.

For twenty-seven years, these businesses held forth on Circuit Avenue, serving meals, drinks, and plenty of music and sports. They were *the* places to hang out on Circuit Avenue for nearly three decades. In 2013, however, both businesses closed, and the site became Ryan's Amusements, aka The Game Room.

Café Moxie

Ninety percent of new restaurants don't last more than five years; Dry Town Café operated from 1995 to 1998—prior to that, the site on the corner of Center and Main Streets Vineyard Haven was the Linden Tree Café. Tina Miller opened Café Moxie in 1998 and "sold it after my second son was born, a bit too much, two little boys and a restaurant." She said, "All fun while it lasted."

Paul Currier and his wife, Cindy Curran, ran Café Moxie for seven years, selling to Austin Racine and Katrina Yekel in May 2008. The young couple had met five years earlier when both worked at Moxie. They were thrilled to take over the business, with Austin the chef and Katrina running the front of the house.

"I feel really good about Austin," said Currier. "A lot of people think they can, but he really can. Owning a restaurant is a little bit like falling in love, but you have to get real. You have to be fastidious, and you have to watch the food costs. Austin is young, but he's disciplined enough to hold all the pieces together."[41]

Before they opened the doors in 2008, Austin and Katrina renovated the facility. On opening night, they graciously greeted their guests, pouring complimentary champagne.

Too soon, disaster struck. Austin Racine was on site on July 4, 2008, when fire erupted at Café Moxie. The conflagration gutted the building and severely damaged the adjacent Bunch of Grapes bookstore. That was a cataclysmic end to the young couple's efforts at Moxie.

In 2012, Mike Ryan assumed ownership and ran the business until 2014, when he sold to Mad Martha's Ice Cream. Today, Chef Spring Sheldon runs S&S Kitchenette at the site, with pop-up dinners and take-away meals. She also operates the El Gato taco food truck.

Captain's Table

The long, narrow building across from the police station in Oak Bluffs, now a bike rental shop, was once home to the Captain's Table. Rick LaPierre bought the Captain's Table in 2002.

Reporter/photographer/musician Mark Lovewell enjoyed breakfast at the Captain's Table in 2005. It was the place in town to go for breakfast, where the food was good, the atmosphere intriguing, and the camaraderie was akin to a place where everybody knew your name. If you were a regular, that is.

LaPierre prided himself on his home fries, which were a little spicy. And apparently there was a bit of spice in the T-shirts he collected—slightly off-color. LaPierre had more than fifty at last count.

Dairy Maid

Big Cronig's in Vineyard Haven is located on the site where little Dairy Maid sat, years ago, serving soft-serve ice cream. Fred Glodis's parents ran the operation.

Darling's

(See chapter 13, "Sweets")

David's Island House

"David Crohan is a homegrown Island celebrity and an institution in his own right," wrote Julia Wells in the *Gazette*. David ran his Island House on Circuit Avenue from 1978 to 1997. Born blind, David Crohan began in "the early days, playing in Circuit avenue bars in the 1960s, to the 20 years that he owned David's Island House and played the piano seven nights a week." He has retired to Florida, but still keeps playing, still going after all these years.[42]

David's Island House was on Circuit Avenue where 11 Circuit is today, a restaurant run by Ralston and Maevis Francis.

The Dunes at Katama Shores Inn

In Katama, where the Winnetu is today, was one of the few year-round restaurants of the 1960s. Most Vineyard restaurants "rolled up the sidewalks," JoAnne Murphy recalled.

JoAnne's mother, Ernestine, was a waitress at the Dunes from 1963 to 1968. She has fond memories of her days at the Dunes when everyone worked together. Islanders who wanted a night out converged at the Dunes, as it was the only show in town. On Friday and Saturday, they had a band, and Ernestine could make $100 a night.

Tony Medeiros often stopped by the restaurant. Policemen in the off-season did not have a lot going on, so officers would drop in for a cup of coffee. One night Officer Medeiros came by when Ernestine was topping pies with whipped cream. Tony startled her; she spun around, squirting him with whipped cream. Tony and his partner took her out and into the backseat of the cruiser. That was memorable.

Three of Ernestine's daughters worked at the Dunes, first as busgirls, then salad girls.

The Thanksgiving menu was extensive at the Dunes. Appetizers included fresh cherrystones on the half shell, shrimp cocktail, or Quahaug chowder. Entrées ranged from oven-roasted turkey to bay scallops and Lazy Lobster. Whipped potatoes and creamed onions were among the vegetables offered, with desserts of baked Indian pudding with ice cream, hot gingerbread with whipped cream, or hot mincemeat pie à la mode. Dinner was served from 1:30 to 8:00 p.m. The price of an entrée was $6.50 and up. *The Grapevine*, precursor to the *MV Times*, featured this promotion in 1977, the good old days.

If $6.50 sounds excessive, the VFW in Oak Bluffs offered a complete turkey dinner for $3.95 that same year. Diners chose dark or white meat, mashed potatoes, or candied sweet potatoes.

When the Atwoods, owners of the Dunes, closed the restaurant, many staff migrated to Louise Tate King's Restaurant on Upper Main Street, Edgartown, at the current site of Atria.

Eagleston Tea House

The site of the Eagleston Tea House was unique. In the era of Island trolley cars, 1872 to 1918, the teahouse was poised by the Lagoon drawbridge between Oak Bluffs and Tisbury. The bridge could not support the electric trolley cars of the early twentieth century; the Eagleston was busy with trolley traffic on the Tisbury side of the bridge.

For many people, this picturesque stop became an outing in itself, as Gene Baer recalled. "The Tea House met the gastronomical delights of passengers who had to wait for the competing trolley. Thus, the bridge served as a literal dividing line between the two trolley lines. The Eagleston Tea House was destroyed in the hurricane of 1944."[43]

Feasts

Feasts of Chilmark opened at the Chilmark Tavern in 1983, although it had previously been located by the courthouse in Edgartown. Jaimie Hamlin and Ray Schilcher ran Feasts. Liz Witham recalled working as a hostess with Maggie Gyllenhaal, the actress. One waitress recalled emptying Michael J. Fox's ashtray at Feasts. This was a fine restaurant for the Up Island crowd. Jimmy Parr printed T-shirts for Feasts when he worked at Wood Chips in Vineyard Haven.

Ray Schilcher relocated to Oak Bluffs, where he opened the Oyster Bar, at the site of Rockland Trust Bank today.

Harborside Inn Restaurant

The restaurant was initially called the Captain's Table when it opened in 1971 and was renamed the Harborside Inn Restaurant in 1984.

After studying at the Culinary Institute of America, Island-born Barbara Fenner was the head chef at the Harborside Restaurant for many years. She left there to partner with Hugh and Jeanne Taylor at the Outermost Inn, where she was in charge of the kitchen, preparing meals for nine years, until her family purchased the Menemsha Galley.

The Harborside closed in 2010 and was replaced by the Atlantic Fish and Chophouse.

Helios

In the early 1960s, when Lucia Moffett lived in Greenwich Village, she met an artist, Bill Prokos, of Greek heritage. They fell in love and moved to Martha's Vineyard in 1968.

Prokos was familiar with Greek cooking, and the "Washashore" couple soon became known around town as the most proficient of Greek cooks. They efficiently prepared moussaka, lamb shish kebab, Greek salads, and honey almond cakes. Their booth at the Agricultural Fair popularized Greek fare.

Initially, Lucia and Bill set up a tiny Greek café on Mayhew Lane in Edgartown. Outdoor tables and an indoor warmth enveloped everyone who stopped by. Beginning with the basics of Greek cooking, they gradually grew their restaurant with a broader menu and wider following. One of the attractions, besides Lucia's warm welcoming, was their espresso machine, one of the first on the Vineyard.

By the mid-'70s, Helios had outgrown itself. James Taylor had built a repair shop, the Nobnocket Garage, at the corner of State and Holmes Hole Roads. When the car repair business failed, Taylor opened the building to local craftspeople and artisans, the Art Workers Guild. And Helios expanded into the converted space, now open year-round. Diners enjoyed summer meals on the porch and in a cozy building in winter.

The Black Dog closed for the winter of 1975, and fans and chef Don Patrick migrated to Helios in the off-season. Chef Patrick had former Black Dog customers' breakfasts ready for them when they pulled in to Helios.

Bill and Lucia returned the favor to the Black Dog the following year when they hosted Greek Night at Black Dog ethnic evenings. Besides an extensive Greek menu, Greek dancing was encouraged at the Black Dog, as it was at Helios.

Joanne Lambert shared fond memories of doing prep work in the kitchen at Helios. "My friend Bill Ochman was one of the cooks, I don't think he was THE chef. He was a character, though! We would go in there because we knew him, and other characters who went there. The belly dancer Diane Hartman danced through the room, with people throwing money at her."

By the mid-1970s, Lucia and Bill had created a unique community at Helios, where Islanders savored the camaraderie that embraced every guest.

Valerie Reese recalled, "Helios was magical, due in no small part to Lucia's charisma, her insistence on quality and authenticity and beautiful presentation. She was also the first person I knew who valued and sought out fresh and local, buying produce and flowers from Arrowhead Farm, fish from local fishermen and milk and cream from Fred Fisher at Nip 'n' Tuck."

In her retrospective of Helios, Valerie described the wide net that drew local diners to the unique atmosphere of Helios. "Our clientele, among others, were artists, musicians, boatbuilders, big-wigs, old money, new money, misfits and stars, along with a motley collection of waifs and strays." One of the regulars came for breakfast straight from his bedroom, clad in robe and slippers.[44]

Onetime employee Julia Mitchell, of West Tisbury, recalled, "Lucia lived her life as though her life was simply about helping people."

Helios reached its prime, serving the likes of Rose and Bill Styron, Beverly Sills, and Lillian Hellman and catering meals for Katharine Graham at Mohu on Lambert's Cove Road.

Bill Prokos passed in 1977, and Helios closed shortly thereafter. However, as noted in *Edible Vineyard*, "Helios occupied a singular place in Martha's Vineyard restaurant lore, a place where art, dining, and belly dancing intersected, a place that was a part of the Vineyard's coming of age in the Seventies, a restaurant for the Age of Aquarius."[45]

Humphrey's

(See chapter 15, "Historic Restaurants")

Kapigan Diner

What remains of the Kapigan Diner is tucked behind the old red gas pump on North Road near Tea Lane. You have to be really old to have stopped by the Kapigan Diner. A long time ago, when Bill Smith of Chilmark was about four or five, the Kapigan closed. Smith recalled, as a wondrous child, peering into the store cases at the Boston crème pies, his mouth watering.

Labelle's

This restaurant was on Circuit Avenue, near today's Murdick's Fudge. As a teenager, Jocelyn Coleman Walton worked there one summer. Because she was Black, she washed dishes in the back of the building because Blacks were not permitted to interact with white patrons.

Lattanzi's

On Church Street, Edgartown, Lattanzi's was a very popular restaurant for decades. In 2013, the owners decided the time was right to close. "So many wonderful people…celebrities, dignitaries, it's been a wonderful journey as far as that goes," Mr. Lattanzi said. "It's like the Seinfeld show. As much as we all loved it, it went out on top. And we were hoping to do the same thing."

Albert Lattanzi ran Lattanzi's for twenty years. "It's very bittersweet because we love our customers, and we love making pizzas for them."

Lawry's

This was on upper Main Street, Edgartown. Betty, the chef, made the best baked stuffed shrimp and scallop stew, but she never shared her recipes.

Lola's

On the site of Anthony's, Lola's held its own for twenty years, nestled between Farm Neck Golf Course and the Island Inn. The highlight of the menu was Cajun cuisine, real southern cooking, with Chef Kathy Domitrovich. The highlight of the building was the colorful mural of dancers.

Mimi Torchin recalled Lola's fondly. "I loved Lola's mostly Cajun cuisine and seafood menu and had many wonderful Thanksgivings there with a whole turkey (a half for a twosome) and all the fixings. And then all the leftovers went home with you. The owner and chef (Kathy, not Lola, tho!) was convivial and always around to say hello."

Lola's transitioned to Hooked, and now Noman's, acknowledging the uninhabited island off the southwest Vineyard.

Louis'

On State Road across from The Little House, Louis' had the best garlic knot rolls for dipping in marinara sauce. The salad bar, rotisserie chicken, and pizza were very popular too.

Louise Tate King's

Louise Tate King's restaurant was on Upper Main Street, Edgartown, where Atria is today.

Shelley Christiansen fondly recalled Louise Tate King's. Her father "loved the food and was intent on making a reservation there on every summer vacation in the late 60s and 70s." Shelley remembered King's as "a fine dining kind of vibe," but "with a home-y feel." The restaurant was filled every night all summer.

Louise Tate King herself met everyone at the door and treated them like royalty. Previously, she had a restaurant at her home in West Tisbury across from Green's Farm. She always had a float in the Edgartown parade with a king on it.

The eatery was known for its frog legs and chocolate mousse. Two chefs kept the food moving.

And Ernestine waited tables there in the late 1960s; each waitress had her own busgirl. She recalls the strict dress code for waitresses, with a white doily on her head, a white apron, a white collar, and a black dress. "She always checked we wore nylons," Ernestine recalled. The joke among staff was that they catered meals to the prisoners at the nearby jail.

Lou's Worry

On Edgartown's North Water Street, Lou's Worry was a popular Islander hangout. When the Kafe and Colonial Inn were bars, locals gravitated to Lou's Worry to socialize and meet up with friends. It was more invested in camaraderie infused with alcohol than fine cuisine. "Lou's Worry wasn't about eating," said Jessica Burnham. It was a year-round hangout for the Island community.

Manning's Snack Bar

Captain and Mrs. Walter Manning opened a family restaurant near the Gay Head lighthouse in 1961. Manning's Snack Bar was open seasonally and employed family members and locals. The consensus was that the best fried food on the Vineyard was dished out by Walter Manning. He used fresh, clean oil, which made his fried clams the very best. His lobster rolls were a delight. "Their quahaug chowder, lobster sandwiches, fried clams and homemade pies were always favorites. Over the years many Islanders worked for the family and have remained friends."[46]

When Walter Manning closed his shop around 1970, Vineyarders mourned the loss of his delectable eatery.

Mr. C's

Mr. C's held forth right on Circuit Avenue, where Fat Ronnie's is today. Mr. C. had the best steak sandwich on Island. The owner was a large gentleman, too big to get out of his store onto the sidewalk, the story goes. "Mr. C was a big guy who used to sit on a bench and was always smoking a cigar," recalled Mr. Cronig. "Every imaginable thing was sold there."[47] Millie Brigg's ran Frosty Cottage at that site years before.

Nick's Lighthouse

"Nick's Lighthouse had the best chicken wings," recalled Sharon Kelley, who ran The Secret Garden on Circuit Avenue. "It had a low-hanging fishnet ceiling. Originally Nick's was where Ben n Bills is today. The restaurant relocated down Circuit Avenue to the current site of Rockland Trust." Sharon continued, "That's where they made pizza."

Back in the day, you couldn't get pizza in the off-season. Once Giordano's closed, Nick's was the place to go for pizza.

Jessica Burnham also had fond memories of Nick's. She described it as an old school seafood restaurant with low, dark ceilings. Glass balls and crabs hung on the walls, and fishnet draped the ceiling. She recalled her father taking the kids to Nick's for fried clams with vinegar. Ernestine remembered Nick's as serving the best seafood on Island.

Not-O-Way

In 1928, when Helen Manning was nine years old, her father opened the Not-O-Way in Gay Head, now Aquinnah. Today, all that remains are a couple of steps that lead onto the oval by the Cliffs. The restaurant was on the outer circle, across from the Lighthouse, near Helen's house, which still stands.

The Not-O-Way was built by a New Bedford man named Gennochio, who never opened it. "I think he was somebody involved in the rum running or something. He had that look," said Helen.

Helen's mother ran the kitchen. "The dining room was very nice too, because they had plate glass windows that looked out on the Atlantic Ocean."

And there was a long table, "and that long table was always covered with lobsters, cooked lobsters. And you just stand up there and open lobsters and eat them just like you do salted peanuts. So that was great."[48]

Ocean Club

The Ocean Club opened at Five Corners in the summer of 1979, when plans to open a McDonald's on Martha's Vineyard collapsed. Tim Dobel was a chef in the early years and recalled, "It was hip high fashion and had great, great food." Celebrities would fly in, which attracted publicity. "It was nuts and wonderful. I doubt we'll see its like again." That was a special place, with a great raw bar. Very popular.

The Oyster Bar

When Ray Schilcher left Feasts in Chilmark, he opened the Oyster Bar on Circuit Avenue. It was a high-end, popular place to dine. The Oyster Bar had initially been the site of Nick's Lighthouse and was succeeded by Rockland Trust Bank.

Papa's Pizza

Primo Lombardi opened Papa's Pizza on Circuit Avenue in 1978. Jeff Lambert worked there for three years around 1990. "Primo was there every day. I respected Primo's work ethic, what he was willing to do. He walked the walk." Jeff went on, "We were the hottest show in town, competing with Giordano's." Primo was generous and appreciative. "Going to work was so much fun," he added.

"It's always been a fantastic family place, a great place for kids," said Deborah Mayhew of West Tisbury, who came out for dinner with her nine-year-old daughter, Katie Ann. "There are so many high-priced, chichi restaurants here, the locals can't afford to eat out anymore. There aren't many left that cater to families and stay open year-round."[49]

Besides pizza, Papa's offered salads and Italian dishes at what once was the A&P, whose mosaic is still in the entryway of the current Beetlebung coffee shop. Papa's Pizza closed in 2001.

Portside

Today, Wind's Up, on Beach Road near the drawbridge, is where the Portside Dairy Bar flourished in the 1970s. The Portside had a sloped roof, like a ski chalet, with garage doors on the side. Franky Frank ran Portside with an impressive array of hamburgers and French fries to supplement his soft-serve ice cream. Frank's burgers and fries were the best on the Island at the time, according to Bill Smith and confirmed by many customers.

Donna Leon remembers kayaking across the Lagoon to enjoy the food at Portside. Patricia Boyd suggested, "I always thought that would have been a good drive-in where the girl on skates would come to your car." She added, "Franky Frank made it special."

Richard's Dessert Gallerie

The Gallerie was in the rear of the Ulysses Mayhew House adjacent to the West Tisbury Congregational Church. It opened in 1976 and lasted about a year. Proprietor Richard Lee (1933–2012) was a dancer, an artist, and a restaurateur for a year. According to Richard Skidmore's defining article in *Martha's Vineyard Magazine*, the Gallerie assumed the space previously used by Crane's Chocolates, known for serving ladies' luncheons.

Lee installed his own frame of reference in the surroundings.

"Lee, who had considerable experience as a charming host, hired pie and cake bakers and a chef and launched into the project with his characteristic humor and enthusiasm." The atmosphere of the Gallerie provided Richard Lee the opportunity to display his unique art, reverse glass paintings.

On opening day, the suspense was palpable. Lee welcomed his guests. "As the tea ladies took in the room, their eyes alighted upon whichever strange, shockingly colored painting was nearest, which caused a momentary flutter."

As they surveyed their surroundings, they were taken in, or appalled, by his voluptuous works of art. And "when one of the women at the table went to the bathroom and returned, pandemonium ensued. Lee had (somewhat discreetly) put what many would call pornographic, but might more accurately be labeled pagan, paintings in the bathroom." Some patrons never returned, but the Gallerie carried on.

The menu was as rich as the art, with tasty lamb chops and mouthwatering desserts. However, Lee's personal cuisine was sauceless pasta, cereal, chocolate, and any flavor of ice cream.

The Dessert Gallerie drew a wide swath of Vineyarders, from proper tea ladies to aging hippies. On occasion, diners flew in to savor the art and the delicacies. Bob Gothard acknowledged guests came ostensibly for the art and the food, but the primary attraction was Richard Lee, the host himself.

Geoff Currier described the experience. "Richard's greeting was always warm and welcoming—and never brief. One must 'set a spell' with Richard as his conversations were inspiring, thought provoking, and sometimes electrifying. His humor was ever present."[50]

Tom Hodgson recalled the amazing dining room. He was amused by the rusty bed frame in front of the Gallerie, filled with geraniums. It was, of course, "a bed of flowers."

Daisy Kimberly felt surrounded by Richard Lee's memorable Bosch-like paintings.

Kate Taylor was impressed by Lee's teacup collection and his dolls. Richard painted the dolls in his own inimical style, which drew his diners' attention.

Elise LeBovit considered the Dessert Gallerie more of a salon than a restaurant. Yes, the art was intriguing, the desserts delightful, but it was the clientele she found unique. Conversations created a "Gertrude Stein/Alice B. Toklas vibe to the place."

Lee's reverse glass art overshadowed the succulent chops, native greens, and juicy pies. As Richard Skidmore summarized the Gallerie, "The happening that was the Dessert Gallerie lasted just a brief moment in time but lives on in Island lore. It is the root of Lee's fame and notoriety on Martha's Vineyard."[51]

The Roadhouse

At the age of twenty-two, Tina Miller and her boyfriend drove across country, camping and savoring the dietary delights of the South and Southwest, from local steak in Austin to enchiladas in Santa Barbara. When they reached California, they realized their goal was to return to the Vineyard and open their own restaurant, serving the succulent cuisine they appreciated on their travels.

Tina had worked as a dishwasher at the Midtown Café, in West Tisbury, and later as a line cook, so she thought she knew her way around a restaurant kitchen. That site, formerly the Wayside, was available when Tina returned from her cross-country culinary immersion. (Today it is the site of State Road Restaurant in West Tisbury.)

She offered some well-honed advice: "It is good to be naive at times, assuming the best will happen, if you have a can-do attitude. You can get a lot done without overthinking. That's how the Roadhouse came to be."

Reviewing the culinary atmosphere of nearly forty years ago, Tina recalled, "The Island food scene was quite different in 1989—not many restaurants, and those were very much New England–style dining—Lawry's Seafood, Anthony's, Seasons, and David Ryan's. Up-Island had the Home Port and the Aquinnah Shop."

With youthful confidence, Tina felt comfortable opening the Roadhouse, although, as she realized, she was a cook, not a trained chef. Her goal was to prepare and serve meals that were simple, healthy, and appreciated by the local populace.

Allan Miller offered paternal advice on the import of consistent meals: each dish should always taste just the same. And it should be good. That's the way to guarantee return business, which is the bread and butter of successful restaurants. Tina heeded her father's words.

Securing a four-year lease and a healthy bank loan, with a little local help, Tina got to work, replacing the Formica bar with mahogany and rebuilding the eight tabletops with recycled yellow pine. The Roadhouse sign was locally painted in dynamic red, yellow, and black.

The diner was ready to open.

It may seem impossible that a young entrepreneur could open a restaurant, but for Tina it all came together, and the Roadhouse opened in mid-June 1989. (The printed menus didn't arrive on time, so the staff had to hand-write them, a memorable opening day task.)

For years, the Roadhouse proved a landmark in West Tisbury. For Tina, and her staff and customers, the Roadhouse proved a magical time in their culinary journey.

It was a young staff, with high aspirations and few expectations. High school students surfed by day and washed dishes at night. College students waited tables. A friend's boyfriend's brother cooked. Customers shared camaraderie with staff. People came to savor the atmosphere, enjoy the experience, and support the twenty-something staff and the food they served.

Tina savored the friendships she made at the Roadhouse, with both staff and customers. Her life was shaped by people who counted on her for a paycheck and those who appreciated her culinary and organizational skills to run a restaurant, right in West Tisbury.

After four years, with the lease coming up, it felt time to move on. It was 1992. The staff was growing up and looking for other options. As Tina phrased it in her autobiographical retrospective in *Edible Vineyard*, "Everyone moved on to new chapters in their young lives. As the years have passed, I never stop hearing how much people loved the Roadhouse."[52]

Seaview Bar

Loretta Balla was the mainstay of the Seaview Bar by the Inkwell in Oak Bluffs. Johnny Seaview was the iconic character who haunted the bar and kept the Island attuned to his unique lifestyle through the years.

Lisa Hart recalled, "My favorite memories are of Johnny Seaview dancing in his tailored Western shirts and cowboy hat." She went on, "And Loretta coming out to beat those of us hanging around way too long after last call." It was a sad day when it was time for Johnny to move on.

Slice of Life

In 2004, Pete and Jen Smyth assumed ownership of Slice of Life on Circuit Avenue in what had been the Circuit Café. Over fifteen years, they built a solid reputation of bountiful breakfasts, specialty lunches, and delicious dinners. It became a local hangout for the Island's gourmet crowd. When the building was sold in 2019, Pete moved to Life at Humphrey's in Vineyard Haven.

Stam's Restaurant

Stam's Restaurant was situated on the Vineyard Haven waterfront. It ran from 1956 to 1963.

Rudolf Stam was a chief steward in the Dutch merchant marine during World War II. As chief steward, he oversaw the kitchen and dining programs aboard ship. He worked on ships until 1950 and then moved back to the Island, where he opened a bakery on Main Street, near Brickman's.

Stam bought property at 79 Main and opened Stam's Restaurant. The focus was seafood, with an ethnic option of Dutch East Indian food, such as curry and a rijsttafel dinner. The atmosphere promoted casual dining, especially at the luncheonette, with breakfast in the coffee shop. Dinner was always in the dining room.

"My father was the chef with the cook working for him," said Peter Stam. "And my mother ran the front of the house."

Stam's had thirty-five tables in the dining room and a counter with eight more tables in the coffee shop. The restaurant was only open in the summer. "Back then," Peter recalled, "it was a short season from mid-June to mid-

Peter and Nancy Stam live in what was once his parents' popular restaurant. *Courtesy of Peter Stam.*

STAM'S Restaurant
Overlooking Vineyard Haven Harbour

LOBSTER   STEAKS   SHRIMP

BIRTHDAY CAKES *Made to Order*

OPEN 7 A. M. to 9 P. M.   CLOSED SUNDAY, 1:30 P. M.
TEL. V. H. 752W

Stam's was a popular Vineyard Haven seafood restaurant in the late 1950s. *Courtesy of Peter Stam.*

September." The family promoted the restaurant with ads in the *Vineyard Gazette* and of course a sign at the Main Street location.

Peter has fond memories of his parents' restaurant. "I was quite young but loved to make the fresh donuts, watching them flip in the circular donut fryer. In the last year I occasionally worked the counter in the coffee shop. I also sometimes ran the potato peeler on the back porch to make French fries."

When Mr. Stam closed the restaurant in 1964, he converted the building into apartments, as it remains today. Peter and Nancy live in the main house and rent out two apartments in the rear.

Looking back sixty years, Peter Stam recalled, "Top memories include running the donut machine, then walking trays of donuts over to the Islander before its first trip of the day." He enjoyed "the activity on a busy evening, filling jelly crullers, getting a chocolate milk directly from the driver of the Whiting's milk truck and getting a hamburger anytime." Enduring memories.

Stams Redux

The restaurant business skipped a generation in the Stam fam, but look for Wicked Burger in the strip mall across from Stop & Shop in Edgartown, opening in 2024. Chris Stam described his eatery as "a straightforward, delicious, grab-it-on-your-way-to-the-beach restaurant."[53] With a veggie burger option! Who could ask for anything more?

Stand-By Diner

This diner was across from the current Oak Bluffs Police Station, in the narrow building that is currently a bicycle rental shop. Rick LaPierre worked at the Stand-By before he bought the Captain's Table, in 2002, in the same building.

Wannacum Inn

Dan Issokson recalls that the Wannacum Inn was on Old County Road in West Tisbury in the late '70s to early '80s. The chef, Mrs. McClure, was a great cook. She claimed that cooking was her hobby. Her specialty was a roast beef dinner, served family-style with all the fixings.

Dan said, "My dad must have taken us there probably between 1967 and 1971." He remembers Mrs. McClure's son, Dale, who played on the football team.

John Goldthwait spent summers in the 1970s cooking at the Harbor View Hotel in Edgartown. When he learned to cook, he said procedure preempted ingredients. "There was no internet, it was just the technique of cooking which made it work."

In the spring of 1974, the cast and animated sharks from *Jaws* were housed on Harbor View property, recalled John. "The cast of *Jaws* had their own baker and chef." He remembered the hired help was put up at the Harbor View as well.

John's college roommate, George Gamble, spent his twenty-first birthday at The Kafe, where you could walk from Main Street through to Among the Flowers, which George and his late wife, Susan, ran for decades.

Fifty years ago, in October 1974, George Gamble was bartending at the Harbor View. It was the last day of filming *Jaws*. The cast was winding down after an exhausting schedule.

In the dining room, someone innocuously tossed a roll that bounced off the table. The recipient responded in kind. Quickly, the room erupted in a certified food fight. Roy Schneider was in it. Richard Dreyfuss threw a gob of food. Steven Spielberg launched a bit of his dinner. And Robert Shaw unloaded. Yes, they were blowing off steam, but they created havoc.

The dining room host was beside herself. The manager was angry at the frivolity and the mess.

The next night, Gamble was tending bar when a reporter for the *National Enquirer* showed up, offering $50 to talk about the previous night's mayhem. Gamble checked with his boss, Bob Carroll. "Ask for $100," said Carroll, "and tell him anything he wants to know."

George Gamble thought the silliness of the food fight proved the movie would be a flop, a dud and would never amount to anything.

My last carnivore meal was on my daughter Amy's sixteenth birthday in 1991. It was an omelet with ham. During the pandemic, she inspired me to try intermittent fasting. I find it does give me more energy and helps (a bit) to keep weight and cholesterol in check. However, I do break it on occasion.

11

BEVERAGES

For years, Island character Jay Schofield drove around with a coffee mug secured to the roof of his car. When someone pointed out the mug, Jay feigned surprise and then pulled a cord, which tipped the mug. Thanks for the memories, Jay!

Who named Martha's Vineyard?

Bartholomew Gosnold, an English captain, sailed from Falmouth, England. "On May 21, 1602, he and his crew of 32 arrived on the shores of an island off the coast of Cape Cod. He observed many vines covering the island (the same varieties that can be seen today) and dubbed the tiny island Martha's Vineyard after his daughter."[54] So far so good.

Although visitors who dote on the grape may be disappointed, it turns out that Vineyard vines do not bear grapes that are good for making wine.

Gosnold later led the Virginia Company to found Jamestown plantation, the first permanent settlement by the English in the New World. He died in 1607 at the age of thirty-six; the new leader was John Smith.[55]

Now it is time for a few brews and a taste of Vineyard wine.

The Ritz Café

Many Vineyard sights and scenes have changed over the years, noted Doug Cabral, former editor of the *Martha's Vineyard Times*, but "among the last remaining holdouts is the Ritz Café, which—along with the cliffs, the beaches, and the ponds—has held the line. A modest watering hole that islanders depend on after the day's work is done and the summer crowds have evacuated to the mainland…has acquired the patina of legend."

Cabral commented on the rugged structure of the Ritz but noted once a visitor steps inside this bar, the laid-back experience greets all comers.

It was built in 1930 as the Topside, and Richard Pease became proprietor of the Ritz Café in 1944. A few tables and chairs filled the room, with pool tables up the steps in the former Topside.

In the '40s, only Edgartown and Oak Bluffs served liquor. Pease ran the Ritz for twenty years, transferring the common victualer's license to Herbert Combra in 1964, with the right to sell alcohol year-round.

Combra added Helen's Grill to serve seafood and short-order meals, seating forty diners. He painted the walls and ceiling and added brass fixtures and seats with chrome and plastic upholstery.[56]

Arthur "Lanky" Pachico, an earth-moving machinery operator, bought the Ritz from Combra in 1967. The Ritz welcomed Islanders of every breed and brand, including the likes of Oliver Perry, aka Johnny Seaview, former horse jockey and Seaview bartender, who hitchhiked around the Vineyard with his chainsaw to cut up trees.

When Lanky passed in 1986, his stepdaughter, Janet King, assumed management. She revamped it into a dance hall that welcomed the likes of Johnny Hoy and the Bluefish with booming bass and bluesy harmonica. The Ritz personality changed dramatically.

Johnny Hoy recalled his early years with the wild dancing. "There were a bunch of skunks living under the floor.…If the floor started bouncing—even when they were hibernating in the winter—you'd make them nervous, and they'd let it go. I mean the place—if it was a hot night—the floor would start to move, and then the next thing it was like, gah! It would reek. As a band, you really knew you had it going when the skunks let it go."

Larkin Stallings, a California native who arrived on the Vineyard by way of Texas, bought the Ritz in 2014. He was quoted as saying, "You know, most of the businesses, most of the restaurants and the bars on Martha's Vineyard have gone through lots of owners over not so many years. This place, though, had gone through very few owners over a long, long period of time."

And Stallings is pleased with his culinary offerings. "Chef Canieka and The Loud Kitchen is up and running. She is fun and just a little bit crazy. Perfect fit for The Ritz."

The Ritz is still a dive bar, but the meals bring a legitimacy and flavor to the atmosphere. Stallings says you never know who will come in and sit down at the Ritz. "It's a place where you can come in no matter who you are, sit down, and you may just be sitting next to an actual commercial fisherman, a working man. Or you may be sitting next to Larry David, and it just works. We have no pretension about who we are. We don't pretend that we're fancy."[57]

Bad Martha's Farmer's Brewery

Bad Martha Farmer's Brewery was founded in 2013.

In brewing craft beer, Bad Martha uses hand-picked wild grape leaves grown on the Vineyard. The first two ales brewed and sold in 2013 were Vineyard Summer Ale and Martha's Vineyard Ale. The brewery offers approximately fifty varieties, with such flavors as fruits, berries, beach plums, honey, oysters, chocolate, and coffee. Beer is brewed on Island, but canning takes place in Falmouth. The brewery has a seven-barrel brewing system.

Bad Martha's tasting barn opened in 2014, with the Napa Valley tradition of wine tasting rooms for consummate connoisseurs. The beer garden atmosphere, with indoor and outdoor seating, is welcoming. Cheese plates, charcuterie, crudité, and pizzas supplement the imbibing.

Jonathan Blum, the owner, sells the beer on Martha's Vineyard, in Falmouth, and throughout Cape Cod, identified by a logo of a dark-haired mermaid. Bad Martha's mission is "to create excellent craft beers and be a socially-responsible company that puts the community first." A portion of profits is donated to the Island Food Pantry.

Offshore Ale

Offshore Ale, the Vineyard's first and only brewpub, opened in 1997 on Kennebec Avenue, in the heart of Oak Bluffs. With nine beer taps and a rotation of twenty-plus selections, the venue offers a range of quality craft beers. The Offshore website proclaims, "Our West Coast Style Lazy Frog

IPA, named for the eponymous game store in Oak Bluffs, helps pay for the maintenance of the Island's disc golf course."

The *Martha's Vineyard Times* checked into the collection of hops used to brew Offshore Ale. Brew master Neil Atkins offered pointers on a current batch from five Island locations. Hopps Farm Road Pale Ale was brewed with hops from the farm of Alan Northcott, in West Tisbury. Another crop was harvested by Gary Montrowl at Cynthia Rigg's Cleaveland House.

A crew of volunteers picked buds from the plants. Apparently hop-growing and picking began as a joke between Northcott and Ken Rusczyk. Today it's a popular activity among friends.

Montrowl was impressed by the crop from the Cleaveland House. The hops were a good-looking selection, vigorous, fresh, and perfectly formed.

Offshore Ale brew master Atkins assessed the hops from Hopps Farm Road. He anticipated they would yield about nine barrels of beer, which is 279 gallons of the Hopps Farm Road Pale Ale.[58]

Chicama Vineyards

"In the 1960s, the Mathiesen family—all eight of them—sailed up the New England coastline. One stop was the Vineyard. It was love at first sight."[59]

> *MARTHA'S VINEYARD, Mass.—There really is a vineyard on Martha's Vineyard. And not a little backyard operation, either. It is a full-scale, no-nonsense, professional operation, and one of these days you are going to see the wine in your local store. Well, maybe not in your local store, but in some stores along the Eastern seaboard.*

So begins an article in the *New York Times* from the fall of 1974, introducing Chicama Vineyards to the world.

The goal was simple: the Mathiesen family planned to make wine.

By 1974, the Mathiesens had planted grapevines over fifteen acres of their land, which spanned parts of Oak Bluffs, Tisbury, and West Tisbury. The *Times* noted, "Demand for Chicama Vineyards wine is purely hypothetical at this point." The only wine on hand was a few five-gallon jars and a small barrel in their barn.

George and Cathy Mathiesen connected with a wine master, Dr. Konstatin Frank. He assured them that the vinifera vine—the backbone of popular vineyards in Europe and California—could succeed in the New England climate. Apprenticing themselves to Dr. Frank, in Hammondsport, New York, the Mathiesens learned the trade. On their second day, however, Dr. Frank fell, breaking his foot. An unintended consequence had George and Cathy harvesting his crop while he oversaw their efforts.

The Mathiesens followed Dr. Frank's advice with the vinifera vines, first planting Chardonnay and Riesling, later Cabernet Sauvignon, Merlot, Chenin Blanc, Pinot Noir, Pinot Gris, Gamay, Gewurztraminer, and a Russian variety called Rkazetelli. Their efforts depended on the Vineyard climate and soil; the future was uncertain.

Sandy soil and moderate climate should be ideal for these grapes, the *Times* observed. The writer compared the Vineyard's growing season favorably with that of Burgundy, France, and better than California's wine country of Napa Valley and Sonoma County.

As Martha's Vineyard is an island with proximity to the Gulf Stream, extreme weather is mitigated.

The Mathiesens planted grape vines over fifteen acres in the early years of Chicama Vineyards. *Courtesy of Lynn Hoeft.*

George Mathiesen monitored grape leaves prior to picking grapes and making wine. *Courtesy of Lynn Hoeft.*

Challenges awaited the Mathiesens' investment of time, money, and effort. A spring frost damaged their crop, so they installed a sprinkler system. Birds devoured grapes; deer invaded their acreage. It was an inauspicious beginning, but the family soldiered on, spending thousands to preserve and protect their precious crop.

Three large fermentation tanks were installed, holding thousands of gallons of wine. Their first bottles were Zinfandel, processed from a ton of California Zinfandel grapes George Mathiesen bought in Boston. Thus, the first bottles of Chicama Vineyards came from California grapes. Once the wines aged, in oak barrels or steel tanks, white wines would be ready for sale, in eighteen months.

The Mathiesens planned to crush eighteen tons of grapes to produce upward of three thousand gallons of wine. All eight Mathiesen family members worked the vineyards, the fields, the winery, or the front shop. Daughter Lynn (Hoeft) designed an image of a seagull, the Chicama Vineyards motif.

The Vineyard has a major drawback. It's hard to get supplies. Every element in making wine must be transported by ferry, which adds time and expense. That's life on an island.

George Mathiesen said it all: "Martha's Vineyard has three important assets for us: the kind of living we enjoy, the right climate for our wine and strangely enough, a market."

With 40,000 summer visitors in 1974, approaching 140,000 in 2024, a ready market of eager customers sought local product. Word of mouth is the best promotion, whether a restaurant or a winery. Summer tourists shared their favorite wine with friends and brought more business.

Toward the end of their first summer, the Mathiesens held an open house for the locals. More than five hundred people showed up, curious and supportive of their new neighbors. Mathiesen was impressed by his efforts. He credited his family, proud, "because we are trying to do it all ourselves. My wife has always been interested in growing and I learned something about finance and management in the corporate world. We have a partnership in fact." He had no qualms about his decision to leave a broadcast executive position for a family enterprise.

And that was how Chicama Vineyards was reviewed and encouraged by the *New York Times*.[60]

A year later, the Mathiesens began to cork bottles of wine. Chicama Vineyards became the first winery ever licensed in the commonwealth of Massachusetts.

The Mathiesens added artisanal baked goods, jams, and jellies to supplement the costs of running the winery. In 1985, they petitioned and prevailed with the Bureau of Alcohol, Tobacco, and Firearms to create a distinct viticultural area (a vineyard) on Martha's Vineyard.

The wine-making process at Chicama Vineyards was very precise. And very popular. *Courtesy of Lynn Hoeft.*

All six children worked the vineyards at various times. "The passion was contagious and soon spread to their children and customers alike," wrote Julia Rappaport in the *Vineyard Gazette*. "Whether it was out in the fields among the grape vines, around the dinner table sampling and critiquing various wines or behind the cash register at the wine shop, every Mathiesen left a mark on Chicama Vineyards."[61]

Some days as many as three or four hundred people would stop by. Tim Mathiesen suggested people visited Chicama Vineyards to relate to the people who grew the grapes for the wine in the bottle on their table. The opportunity to visit a thriving vineyard, on Martha's Vineyard, was unique.

Meeting and chatting with the wine makers pleased many customers over the years. "I will never forget the welcoming energy as we walked up to the winery—we sampled only and bought 2 bottles—1 to drink and 1 bottle to take home for the memory—I am looking at the second bottle right now," wrote one customer, years later.[62]

The Mathiesen family operated Chicama Vineyards more than three decades, a vineyard in the heart of Martha's Vineyard.

In 2001, the Mathiesens sold four acres to the Martha's Vineyard Land Bank. George Mathiesen died in 2005; Catherine passed in 2007. With their parents' deaths, the next generation pondered the winery's future. No one wanted to work the winery on their own.

Julia Rappaport concluded the Mathiesens' saga of Chicama Vineyards.[63]

In 2008, "The big wooden doors of the Chicama Vineyards shop closed for the last time Sunday evening at two minutes past five. The shelves of the shop, once stocked with wines made from the grapes grown outside and vinegars infused with that wine, were empty, or nearly so. Hundreds of people stopped in over the weekend to celebrate the end of an adventure in farming and business begun 37 years ago by the late George and Catherine Mathiesen."[64]

While the closing itself was festive, it marked the end of an era.

Tim Mathiesen acknowledged, proudly, that his parents had lived their dream into their eighties, fulfilling a career path as wine stewards. Chicama Vineyards had met his parents' goals.

Lynn (Mathiesen) Hoeft contacted other New England wineries to sell their equipment, the harvesting tools, the bottle line. She was gratified to give new life to what had served the family.

In May 2008, the first licensed winery in Massachusetts sold its last bottles of wine after a very successful run.

One of my favorite meals was the one Dick Goodell and I prepared together for our spouses and friends Jay and Pat Schofield. The theme was Italian. We began with an antipasto, mounded with greens, cheese, salami, tomatoes, olives, and Italian dressing. The main course was homemade linguine, of which Dick is a master. The red sauce was accompanied by braciole, a thin-sliced steak filled with a combination of parmesan cheese, hard-boiled egg, parsley, and pine nuts. The steak is rolled up and tied, seared, and simmered in red sauce.

Dessert consisted of a chocolate log cake filled and frosted with a mascarpone frosting. Another treat was puff-dough pastries filled with Nutella. Our aperitif was limoncello.

The dinner was a hit!

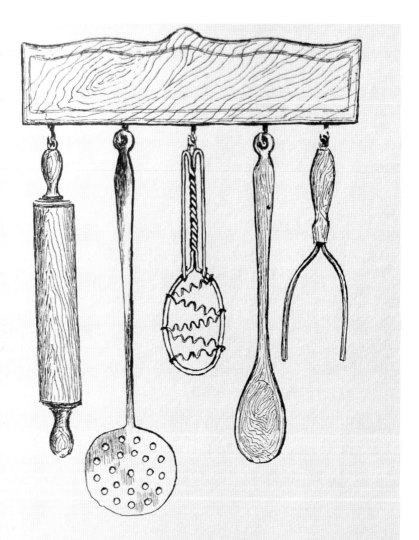

Pies, Puddings, and Other Desserts

Chapter 9

The *Martha's Vineyard Cook Book* (1971) features a variety of meals, from colonial dishes to ethnic options. And desserts. *Courtesy of* The Martha's Vineyard Cook Book.

12

JUST DESSERTS

Not so many years ago, a character arranged day-old Dunkin' Donuts to be shipped to Martha's Vineyard. The cad sold them, right on Circuit Avenue, for a couple of weeks. So, there was a Dunkin' Donuts on the Vineyard until authorities got wind of his caper and shut it down.

*D*esserts were not commonly served in the colonial era, except on special occasions or for guests. Most desserts consisted of fruits or sweetened corn. Apple pies were baked in winter but not necessarily as a dessert. With a dearth of hunting and fishing, stored apples, or pumpkins or squash, were cut up and served as a pie. Also, Brown Betty was a popular dish comparable to a pie, with layers of apples and breadcrumbs.

Slumps, grunts, and brambles were essentially fruit based, topped with biscuit dough. The dish was covered and cooked, steaming the ingredients. Another dessert, mixing blueberries or blackberries, often with whipped cream, was called a fool.

Tina Miller is no fool. She is a certified foodie, gaining experience and sharing meals with the Island populace over the years. She ran The Roadhouse (1987–1991) and Café Moxie (1998–2001). She is co-editor of *Edible Vineyard* and author of *Vineyard Harvest: A Year of Good Food on Martha's Vineyard* (2005).

Tina appreciates the dining experience. "Food memories are long-lasting and emotional. Maybe that's why many old-fashioned recipes stay in demand: they bring us back to a familiar and comforting place and time." She generously shared her popular Roadhouse Gingerbread recipe.[65]

Roadhouse Gingerbread, with Dark Rum Sauce
Beloved by the late Trudy Taylor

2 sticks butter, melted
½ cup granulated sugar
1 egg
2½ cups flour
1½ teaspoons baking soda
1 tablespoon ground cinnamon
1 tablespoon ground ginger
½ teaspoon salt
½ cup dark molasses
½ cup honey
1 cup boiling water
½ cup confectioners' sugar
2 tablespoons dark rum

Preheat the oven to 350 degrees. Grease a 9×12-inch baking pan.

Using a stand mixer or a handheld electric beater, beat the melted butter, granulated sugar, and egg together. Add the flour, baking soda, spices, and salt. Mix briefly to combine. On low speed, add the molasses and honey, then slowly add the boiling water. Mix until combined. Pour into the prepared pan.

Bake for 30 minutes or until a knife or toothpick comes out clean. It serves eight people.

Blend the confectioners' sugar and rum thoroughly and pour the sauce over the top of the warm cake (right in the pan) before serving.

Another recipe for a delicious dessert was submitted by Joyce for a cookbook, published by Sacred Heart Parish, in recognition of the Oak Bluffs centennial, in 1980.

Chocolate Intrigue Cake

Sift Together

3 cups sifted all-purpose flour
2 teaspoons baking powder
½ teaspoon salt

Set aside.

Cream 1 cup butter or margarine, thoroughly. Gradually add 2 cups sugar, creaming until light and fluffy.

Blend in 3 unbeaten eggs, one at a time, beating well after each.

Combine 1 cup milk and 1½ teaspoons vanilla

Add alternately with the dry ingredients, beginning and ending with dry ingredients. Blend thoroughly after each addition. With electric mixer use low speed.

Pour ⅔ of batter into 10-inch tube pan, greased on bottom. Add to remaining batter ¾ cup chocolate syrup, ¼ teaspoon soda, ¼ teaspoon peppermint extract, if desired. Mix well. Pour chocolate batter over white batter.

Do not mix!

Bake at 350 degrees for 45 minutes. Place a sheet of foil on top of pan; continue baking 20–25 minutes. Cool completely before removing from pan.

For years, a group of ROMEOS gathered for lunch at Woodland Grill in Vineyard Haven. If I (Tom) were to go in today, Rob would have my grilled cheese, with tomato on wheat, ready for me. Long live Retired Old Men Eating Out.

13

SWEETS

Forrest Gump famously says, "My mama always said life was like a box of chocolates. You never know what you're gonna get."

We offer a sample of chocolates and sweets savored by Vineyarders over the years.

This charming memory of bygone sweets was written about by Phyllis Meras many years ago.[66]

"Miss Priscilla Hancock of West Tisbury never wanted to leave the Vineyard, so she began making fudge." Priscilla Hancock lived on a farm in Chilmark, Quenames. Dozens of people stopped by to purchase chickens or eggs; others traipsed across the family acreage on their way to South Beach. Word of mouth spread of her sweet chocolates across the Vineyard.

The crowds of candy purchasers were immense. "It was almost as bad some days as going to the A&P," Miss Wing, her partner, said. "There were such crowds."

Miss Hancock had two assistants, an experienced chocolate dipper from Boston and a family friend, Mrs. Donald Poole. She used the best ingredients, took her time, and combined intriguing tastes. "I always used sweet chocolate for anything with fruits and nuts in it, but then I'd dip butter creams and peppermints in bittersweet."

Priscilla Hancock shared memories of long-ago West Tisbury with reporter Phyllis Meras. As a child, she concocted her own view of cooking, mixing flour and water, and perhaps other ingredients, to bake mud pies.

Miss Hancock retired from candy-making in 1956 and lived on Old County Road with her partner Miss Wing. "Well," she said, "I guess that I'm willing [to share my recipe] now that I've gone out of business."

Priscilla's Chocolate Nut Fudge

4 cups granulated sugar
1 ½ teaspoons salt
1 ½ cups light cream
2 tablespoons corn syrup
6 squares Baker's unsweetened chocolate
5 or 6 tablespoons butter
2 teaspoons vanilla
1 ½ or 2 cups coarsely chopped nuts (walnuts or pecans)

Bring sugar, salt, cream, and corn syrup to the boiling point and cook slowly for several minutes, then add chocolate. Reduce heat and cook without stirring to soft ball stage or if a thermometer is used to 234 degrees. Put butter and vanilla in mixture; do not stir in when lukewarm; beat to creamy stage. Then add nuts. Makes four pounds.[67]

Darling's

"Darling's was the popcorn-based establishment of probably 60 years with the endearing sign, 'Darling's, For Twenty Years The Best.'" Skip Finley savored his memories of Darling's as a mainstay on Circuit Avenue, with its distinctive aromas. He added, "Darling's puts a smile on the face of probably half of the folks reading this who remember the days when, thanks to the iconic business, Circuit Avenue smelled of popcorn and candy."[68]

A favorite treat was the Darling's flavored popcorn bars. Jessica Burnham of Edgartown recalled eating the popcorn bars as a child; her father had them when he was a child as well. The bars were sticky, solid, crushed popcorn, served in wax paper. On a summer night, it was a treat to ride the Flying Horses and then get a popcorn bar at Darling's.

Darling's opened in 1900 and closed in 1981. Customers fondly recall the motto above the door: "For Twenty Years the Best."

Darling's, the most popular candy shop on the Vineyard, thrived for more than three-quarters of the twentieth century. *Courtesy of Arne Carr.*

Carroll Darling, a summer Vineyarder, grew up in Albany, Vermont, where his father ran Darling's Hotel. Carroll owned the Cary Maple Sugar Company, once the largest such establishment in the country. According to Chris Baer's This Was Then column in the *MV Times*, maple flavoring "was then used principally to flavor plug tobacco and cigarettes."

"Darling's was a successful mainstay of Circuit Avenue for most of the twentieth century. In 1912, Darling exhibited his state-of-the-art motor-driven popcorn and candy machinery at the Boston Electrical Show. In 1924, Darling bought the Eagle Theatre at the base of Circuit Avenue and the iconic storefront was born. Darling's nephew, Harris Carr, inherited the business when Carroll Darling died in 1936, and his son, Arne Carr eventually ran Darling's for years."[69]

In the 1920s, before the Depression, Carroll Darling hired vendors to walk along the beaches of Oak Bluffs and sell his eponymous popcorn and candy. His great-nephew, Arne Carr, recalls his youth, especially, "the early teen years where I would swim till the 4 pm boat came, then rush back to pop the corn."

Arne added, "My grandfather, Frank B. Carr, would come to the Island from the Northeast Kingdom [Vermont], every summer to help cook. He was known as the 'fudge man.'" The Carrs stayed on the second floor of a house at 10 Kennebec Avenue. They used the first floor to store supplies in the manufacture of the popcorn and candy: fifty-five-gallon barrels of corn syrup and big wooden barrels of molasses.

Arne's memory of Darling's is very descriptive of the operations. The store was divided into sections:

The counter area comprised movable, ten-foot-long counters that could stretch out on the main street porch or more casually inside in a loop.

Behind the inside counter area was the taffy-wrapping machine. A large table was adjacent for hand-wrapping peanut taffy and caramels. This was a social area where wrappers sat about the table and hand-wrapped the candy. It was a relaxed atmosphere, away from the crowds.

The corn room, on the north side of the first floor, was loud and quite active with popping, cooking, and grinding popcorn. That's where the corn bars were made. When the corn syrup was cooked, "We hustled to mix the ground popcorn into the deep copper kettle, pack the prepped popcorn mix (vanilla, wintergreen, chocolate, and molasses) into a fashioned wooden tray, then press the popcorn in a pressing machine." That was the dangerous part.

Once the corn was cooked and pressed, "the trays were brought over to the cutting table and quickly, yet with care, run the knife on the cutting guide to produce individual corn bars."

The process continued. Individual corn bars were packed into foot-long tin boxes for storage. "The boxes of corn bars were then opened, and each corn bar wrapped when needed, usually within the week."

Behind the corn room, by the back kitchen, was a concrete "porch" for potato chips. "We had a machine that removed the potato skin, a simple but impressive procedure." The machine was turned by hand, peeling and slicing multiple potatoes. The fryolator was out on the porch too.

In the spring of 1958, Harris Carr put a copper kettle of oil on the stove to heat up and cook raw nuts. Then he walked from Darling's up Circuit Avenue to get the daily newspaper, as was his wont. Along the way, he chatted with people he met. His return was later than usual. The kettle of oil overheated. A fire broke out in the kitchen.

The crisis expanded exponentially. "The back kitchen became inflamed. He apparently went for the outside kitchen door to get an extinguisher and had a heart attack. The kitchen was pretty much destroyed and there was much smoke damage on the first floor to the front. However, with help, we opened the store within two weeks with mainly popcorn products. We progressed from there to producing fudge, caramels and taffy."

Harris Carr died four days before Arne graduated from prep school. "I ran the candy production that year and then went to college. In a few years my mom sold Darling's."[70]

In a *Gazette* piece in 1981, Phyllis Meras reported a fan's recollections of Darling's from her youth: "It was a must when I was a young girl and we came over from New Bedford to go home with Darling's saltwater taffy," Mrs. James A. Boyle of New Seabury, formerly of Vineyard Haven, remembered. "There was that wonderful kind with the nuts in it."

"Peanut taffy was always among the most popular flavors," said Mrs. Harris Carr, whose husband owned Darling's from 1939 until 1958, "but we had 12 other kinds, too," she added proudly, reciting the mouth-watering litany. "Vanilla, chocolate, chocolate cream, peanut, peanut butter center, cloves, cinnamon, anise, lime, molasses, molasses peppermint, molasses nut, peppermint."

Phyllis Meras shared her emotions on the closing of Darling's in 1981 and the transition to Murdick's Fudge: "I heard this week that there will be no more Darling's, the old popcorn store, in Oak Bluffs this summer or any other summer. Murdick's Fudge Kitchen of Mackinac Island, Michigan, will take its place."

While the reporter observed she had nothing against Murdick's Fudge, which had already made inroads on the Vineyard, it wasn't the same. Meras noted her sister-in-law smacked her lips when she heard Murdick's was coming to town. Phyllis Meras concluded, "But Murdick's isn't Darling's, which has sold buttery white popcorn, and popcorn bars, and saltwater taffy on Circuit avenue since the turn of the century."[71]

In a recent *Gazette* piece, more than forty years later, reporter Phyllis Meras recalled chatting with a fellow nonagenarian, Shirley Kennedy, about Darling's, "where we could buy pink wintergreen or white vanilla or brown chocolate popcorn bars, or simply watch the arms of the taffy machine moving up and down making salt water taffy."[72]

Murdick's Fudge

The saga of Murdick's Fudge began in 1887 on an island far from Martha's Vineyard, Mackinac Island in Lake Huron, Michigan. While a couple of sailmakers, Henry Murdick and his son Rome, were building an awning for a hotel, Sarah Murdick opened Murdick's Candy Kitchen, selling her confectionary delight: fudge.

Other fudge makers followed, making Mackinac Island the fudge capital of the country, with thirteen fudge stores. In 1978, the owner of Murdick's established a shop on the Vineyard.

About the expansion to Martha's Vineyard in 1978, Mike McCourt said in 1993, "I'm not sure what it is about islands and fudge shops, but it seems to be a marriage made in confectionary heaven. For people who visit the island, it's almost a required part of their stay." With three down-Island shops, Murdick's continues as a staple in the Vineyard confectionary community.[73]

Chilmark Chocolates

For thirty-five years, from 1984 to 2019, Chilmark Chocolates was the epitome of handmade chocolates on Martha's Vineyard, with cars spilling out onto State Road, patient people waiting by the door, and satisfied customers emerging, faces beaming, chops working their little lump of chocolate.

Located just beyond Beetlebung Corner, the chocolate confectionery was known far and wide. Customers were encouraged to take a sample at the door, then choose which delicious pieces to pack away for future enjoyment and which to eat on the spot. It was always a cheerful group of customers, eager for their treat.

And behind the scenes, but in plain view, worked a range of employees, busily making, boxing, and selling the chocolates. The crew were serious but friendly, dedicated to their employment, amicable to the steady stream meandering through. A debt of gratitude was shared with the co-owners for their dedication to contributing to the welfare of the community.[74]

The co-owners decided the time had come to close down the operation after thirty-five years.

Mary Beth Grady recognized the shop had served its purpose in providing chocolates for the Vineyard community and jobs for

Vineyarders, many with disabilities. The owners opted not to sell but simply to close their doors.

Allison Berger said, "While she will miss the customers, she worried a little about the employees—many of whom have a variety of disabilities. It has long been part of the store's unique business model to train and employ people with disabilities."[75]

The era of handmade chocolates in Chilmark suffered only a brief break before it was replaced by another unique chocolate establishment.

Salt Rock Chocolates

Growing up near the iconic Chilmark Chocolates, Sarah and Allison Flanders could not avoid sampling the popular confection, following their mother Joy's love. "And that's where our taste for good chocolate began," wrote the Flanders sisters on their website. They explained, "After 10 years of walking through the woods, over a stream and past Chilmark Chocolates on our commute to Menemsha School (now the Chilmark School), we got our first jobs there." Over the years they maintained an interest in chocolate making, recognizing "how chocolate can brighten someone's day and bring people together."

After college and exploration over in mainland America, the sisters felt the Vineyard calling them home. They combined their individual talents, making the whole greater than the two, and established a new chocolate company in Chilmark. Their management and craft skills and local experience evolved into the Salt Rock Chocolate Company, just a year after Chilmark Chocolates closed.

Inauspiciously, they opened their portable door a month after the pandemic closed every door in town. Nevertheless, the Island community welcomed Salt Rock with open, eager mouths.

"The sisters have replicated some of their predecessor's classic recipes such as the ABC (Almond Butter Crunch) and chocolate dipped cranberries." As their website notes, "Our chocolates are influenced by the colors and tastes of the island we grew up on. We love the process of hand-making each chocolate and are excited to share it with you!"[76]

As mentioned before, my mother was in charge of the kitchen, but one day when she was out my Italian grandmother helped me make chicken cacciatore for my college friends. It was delicious, and when I got married, it was the only dish I knew how to make.

You can only eat it so many days in a row though!

14

ISLAND GROWN INITIATIVE

Bob Douglas wanted a dining car on the Vineyard as a café for the Black Dog. He bought a train car and had it dismantled and ferried over to the Vineyard, then reassembled.

To open his café, Douglas needed handicapped access, capacity to expand, and sewer tie-in. He never sought permission, so the train car has stood idle on State Road these past thirty years.

Condiments are the name of the game," said Gail Arnold, a full-fledged foodie. Condiments add to the flavor and taste of any meal. And Gail has a lot more on her plate than salt and pepper.

"I love being part of a community in action: gleaning produce from local farms, stocking the shelves in the pantry, preparing soups, stews and other meals, sharing laughter and stories in and out of the pantry." Gail Arnold is a pantry volunteer and IGI (Island Grown Initiative) board member, as well as the wife of Livingston Taylor and a chef for Steven Spielberg.

Arnold's comments adorn an IGI flyer, promoting its programs to combat food insecurity. The facts speak for themselves: Some 4,200 Islanders are registered with the Island Food Pantry, the highest number in years, more than in the pandemic. Housing costs, transportation issues, and family expenses affect food purchasing. IGI has defined a role for itself on Martha's Vineyard to combat food insecurity. It's all around us. It is real.

Island Grown Initiative has stepped up to work on food insecurity on Martha's Vineyard. Founded in 2006 specifically to address Vineyard food issues, the Hub of IGI is centrally located in Oak Bluffs, near the four-town boundary where Oak Bluffs, West Tisbury, Vineyard Haven, and Edgartown all meet.

The primary source of found food for IGI is its gleaning program.

IGI calculates the pounds of gleaned vegetables. It is an impressive take, for free, from the fields of farms on Martha's Vineyard.

In the early 2010s, IGI harvested less than twenty thousand pounds of veggies a year. In 2022, the number approached fifty thousand pounds and in 2023 topped sixty thousand. Those are amazing statistics and directly attributable to the expanding agricultural acreage available for gleaning *and* the expanding number of volunteers who come out to make this worthy project succeed.

The vegetables are gleaned and cleaned, sorted, and distributed to needy organizations, which in turn distribute this surplus food to families and individuals who benefit from an additional, and inexpensive, food supply. It's a win-win program. Vineyarders appreciate this undertaking.

Island Grown Initiative has done a great deal under the tutelage of Rebecca Haag. She said, "Since 2006, Island Grown Initiative has led an innovative, collaborative effort to increase local food production, reduce food waste, promote climate-friendly farming techniques, and expand access to healthy, affordable food throughout the Martha's Vineyard community."

Island Grown Initiative promotes four essentials to Island life: education, housing, healthcare, and food security. IGI focuses on food. IGI is known for growing, gleaning, cooking, and distributing food across the Vineyard. And since IGI now operates the Island Food Pantry, more vegetables are available for those in need,

Rebecca Haag has been the executive director of IGI since 2016. When queried about the organization, she said, "Simply put, we are the food people on the Island."

Haag elaborated on different elements of IGI. There is a concerted focus to develop regenerative agriculture that can influence the climate in a positive way, reducing our collective carbon footprint. Developing healthy soil holds minerals and absorbs water, two mainstays of regenerative agriculture. Plant rotation, cover crops, and poking a seed in the ground instead of plowing a furrow improve the soil. Such techniques are under the auspices of Andrew Woodruff, who, since 2006, has been the head of the Hub, the organization's forty-acre farm on Stoney Hill Road, Oak Bluffs.

Now IGI has a composting station for food waste. The food-waste program is implemented at the Agricultural Fair; it is the accepted means of recycling food we no longer need or want. Compost enriches the soil.

Education is imperative. IGI teaches students in the schools, farmers in fields, and homeowners in gardens. The impact on the younger grades is impressive. They learn where their food comes from and literally watch it materialize in their school gardens, in place at each elementary school.

For those who need land to plant and harvest their own vegetables, Backyard Growers rents garden plots at the Hub. Water and compost are provided to the neat, sunny acres, perfect for the amateur or the expert. The seed-sharing program is tied in to Polly Hill Arboretum. Community Workshops educate and improve gardening skills.

IGI is known for its gleaners, volunteers who go into the fields and harvest the crops to be shared with those in need. The program has expanded over the years, encompassing young people as well as seniors, a real feel-good program, where the compensation is not just the extra veggies volunteers get to take home but also the warm feeling of helping someone by putting food on their table.

In the *Vineyard Gazette* in 2022, Tom wrote that "I've been a gleaner for nearly a dozen years. It's not a big deal. I pick veggies local farmers don't need or want. It feels good to be close to

The queen of gleaning, Astrid Tilton, relaxes after another successful harvest. *Courtesy of Thomas Dresser.*

the soil and part of a program that donates food to young and old across the Vineyard.

"Gleaning. We glean excess vegetables primarily at Morning Glory Farm and the Island Grown Initiative Hub. It's out of doors. It's not a lot of heavy lifting. It's energizing. The veggies we harvest range from radishes and beans early in the season to tomatoes and corn in late summer to tubers like potatoes and carrots in late autumn. Island Grown Initiative, under the able direction of Astrid Tilton, delivers the produce to senior centers, elderly housing, the schools, and the Food Pantry. It's a win-win arrangement because the food is used, and appreciated, by everyone.

"When tomatoes or corn are available the demand is great. Potatoes and carrots are not as exciting, but the need is still there, and the fruits of our labors are delivered on a regular basis. When we gather more veggies than people need, IGI re-purposes the produce for later use.

"Our compensation is that we get to take home some of whatever is gleaned. Gleaners come in all ages. We are volunteers and together tackle the day's assignment. Working together makes the project go quickly and the collaboration leads to instant communication. Friendships often blossom on farmers' fields. Over the years I've met many people willing to lend a hand. And no one goes home empty-handed."[77]

Since the Food Pantry merged with IGI, there are now 4,200 people registered to receive food at the Pantry. That's 20 percent of the Island population, which exemplifies the breadth of food shortage on Island. Many are summer residents, struggling with health, aging, or housing issues with limited funds for food.

Rebecca Haag sees herself as "the marketeer, out there with the pompoms raising funds and raising interest." She went on, "I love to eat, I love to cook, but I am not a farmer or an educator." It's the IGI team who make things happen; she's the coach, dreaming up strategies for the team to bring to life.

"For us, food is at the heart of health and wellness."

She concluded, "Food is more than just nutrition. It is also love, it is family, it is community, it is tradition and history." And finally, "Food is related to people feeling connected and loved."[78]

Rebecca Haag feels comfortable with the success of IGI to pass the torch and retire in 2024. Two of her final projects are completion of housing for farm workers at the Hub and opening new facilities for the Food Pantry on

Dukes County Avenue, in Oak Bluffs. Her shoes will be filled by two very capable people, Noli Taylor and Michelle Gittlen. Noli Taylor was a founder of Island Grown Initiative and will direct programs and outreach, while Michelle Gittlen will oversee operations. They make an admirable team to bring IGI to the next level.

When Lynne Whiting retired as president of the board of IGI in 2023, she shared Maya Angelou's poignant phrase "I have found that among its other benefits, giving liberates the soul of the giver." Don't you want to liberate your soul?

> *I wanted a festive event when I turned seventy. We reconfigured our dining room to accommodate daughters, brothers and wives, and close personal friends. It was February, brisk but beautiful. Joyce's lasagna stole the show, making the event most memorable.*

15

HISTORIC RESTAURANTS

*McDonald's tried to open on Martha's Vineyard in the 1970s. Islanders erupted
with an aggressive protest, Ronald McDonald was hung in effigy, and a bumper
sticker circulated that read, "Keep Mac off Martha."*

One element in this culinary history, perhaps most important, is the
continuity of restaurants through the years. Running a restaurant
is a challenging business. Consistent meals, difficulty with supply
shortages, machinery repairs, price increases, staffing, management,
marketing, and a host of related items affect the success of serving meals to
the public.

We congratulate the following restaurants that have built solid
reputations and look back on decades of serving delicious dietary
delights. Each of the top dozen eateries has been in business on Island
more than half a century.

These long-standing emporiums deserve extra credit. We honor their
fortitude in persisting through generations of ownership, management,
cooking, and creating an attractive repertoire of dining, appreciated by the
Island community.

Following are the gold stars, the blue ribbons, the Stanley Cups of
Vineyard dining.

1. The Ocean View House, 1893

It was the summer of '41; a couple of teenagers showed up at the Ocean View Restaurant in Oak Bluffs. State Representative Joseph Sylvia, then proprietor of the Ocean View, recalled the incident.

The teenagers were barefoot and carried a torn sail. "They were as soaking wet as if they had been dropped overboard, their sail was also soaking wet and torn, they had no spare clothing nor even underwear, and explained rather piteously, that they had come from the mainland, bound for Edgartown to race."

The boys had endured a rough crossing of Vineyard Sound and were cared for by the Ocean View staff. Sylvia and his housekeeper, Mrs. Frank Silvia, offered the boys a room with hot showers and dry clothes. Samuel Issokson, a Vineyard Haven tailor, repaired their sail.

"In due time the boys got hungry and wanted food, and we had to hunt them up some shoes and stockings in order to make them presentable in the dining room."

When the teens headed to Edgartown the next day, they were ready to race. And the bill for their stay was paid by the father of one of the young men, John F. Kennedy. As Joseph Sylvia recalled, "But we had no idea that we had been entertaining a future President of the United States."[79]

The father, of course, was Joseph P. Kennedy. And the second fellow was classmate, future PT boat commander, and Congressman Torbert Hart Macdonald.

And the duo made the race in Edgartown. Kennedy and Macdonald sailed JFK's twenty-six-foot *Victura*, winning the Wiannos race of 6.4 miles in 3:11:58, 30 seconds ahead of second-place *Seagle*.

The Ocean View story began years before Kennedy's search for food and shelter. The archival history of the Ocean View House is preserved in the files of the Martha's Vineyard Museum, where accounting records from the late 1880s and '90s are curated for future research.

In the 1860s, Erastus Carpenter and the Oak Bluffs Land and Wharf Company developed Cottage City as the country's first planned summer residential community. One key construction was the Sea View House, by the steamship pier.

The Sea View boasted 125 rooms, with parlors, dining salons, and reception suites. The hotel dominated the harbor, popular with tourists who flocked to the seaside resort in the late 1800s.

On September 24, 1892, the Sea View House burned in a fire ostensibly caused by a steam engine spark. The hotel was destroyed within an hour of the alarm being sounded.

"The Sea View House was truly a preeminent tourist destination and major attraction for thousands of guests. The Sea View House structure may be lost to history, but its spirit of hospitality and recreation is alive and well."[80]

The facility was rebuilt as the Ocean View House in 1893 by Benjamin and Mary Rice, operators of the Sea View. It was situated on the far side of Lake Anthony, by The Highlands. Rooms offered a view of the lake before it was opened to the ocean and became Oak Bluffs Harbor in 1900.

Benjamin and Mary Rice, the proprietors of the Ocean View House, bought most of their food supplies in Cottage City, as Oak Bluffs was known at the time. Their meals were locally sourced.

The Rice family operated the Ocean View House nearly half a century. Benjamin passed in 1902, and Mary followed twenty years later; their son and daughter, Frank and Elizabeth, continued to operate the facility well into the 1930s.

Frank Rice died of a heart attack at sixty-four in April 1938. "Death came as he completed the making of some ice cream for the Triad Club which was meeting there." When Frank Rice passed, his sister, Elizabeth, sold the facility to Representative Joseph Sylvia.[81]

Sylvia doubled the restaurant to 120 seats. In 1954, supported by Loretta Balla of the Seaview, he opened a cocktail lounge in the basement. The atmosphere was enhanced by wrought-iron furniture with "gaily-covered plastic fiber seats, tables and chairs scattered about the room." Included in the renovations were restrooms, an ice-making machine, and air-conditioning.[82]

Representative Sylvia sold the Ocean View to Gene and Grace Porter in 1956. The *Gazette* commended the Ocean View as one of the more historic hostels, dating to the early days in the town's history. And the newspaper praised the Rice family as pioneers in the hospitality of the town in its incubation period.[83]

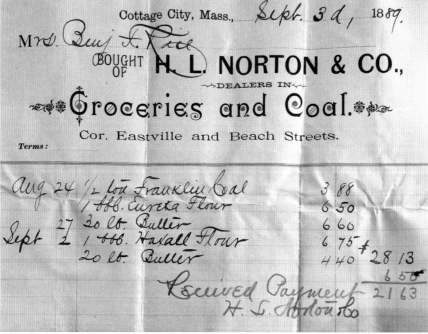

Top: This postcard of the Ocean View House is reminiscent of the impressive hotels of bygone years. *Courtesy of the Oak Bluffs Library.*

Bottom: In the 1890s, Benjamin and Mary Rice ran the Ocean View House on Washington Park, Oak Bluffs. They bought most of their produce locally. *Courtesy of the Martha's Vineyard Museum.*

The Ocean View House was one of the last great Island hotels of the late nineteenth century. The Ocean View survived until it succumbed to a devastating fire in January 1965. The facility was rebuilt only as a restaurant and flourished into the twenty-first century under the Jackson family, who offered a menu of seafood and traditional American cuisine. In 2015, Michael Santoro bought the business, leasing the building from real estate developer Charles Hajjar.

In March 2022, the Ocean View Restaurant again burned. The site was cleared and, at this time, is still vacant. Hajjar plans to rebuild the restaurant in the fall of 2024, with five apartments each on the second and third floors. Hajjar assured town officials he would offer the apartments only to working people on Island. Michael Santoro called the outlook promising. "I'm excited," he said. "Hopefully we'll have a brand-new place."[84] Hajjar plans to reopen the Ocean View in the spring of 2025.

2. Giordano's Italian American Restaurant, 1930

Giordano's Italian American Restaurant in Oak Bluffs is the longest-running family-owned restaurant on Island. In the late 1920s, Edwardo and Maria Giordano settled in East Boston after leaving Avelino, Italy. Edwardo missed his fishing village and wanted to return to Italy, but Maria would have none of that. Around 1930, they visited Martha's Vineyard, and once Edwardo saw the fishing village of Menemsha, he was smitten. They soon moved to Oak Bluffs and bought the Pawnee House, a hotel with a restaurant in the same location as the current Pawnee House.

The Giordanos had a challenge applying for a common victualler's license. At that time, there was, even on Martha's Vineyard, a hesitancy to provide such a license to Italians. However, Maria was quite sharp and applied under the name Mary Jordan. They got the license and were in business. They wanted to offer an extensive menu that included Italian spaghetti and meatballs as well as tuna fish or ham sandwiches.

They named their restaurant Giordano's Italian American Restaurant. Grandson Richie Giordano related how Edwardo had a hot dog cooker that he walked the streets with. The cooker sat in the middle with rolls on one side and condiments on the other. And as he traveled around, he'd sing this song: "They're all ready and they're all red hot, pickles in the middle and mustard on top." He sold hot dogs for a nickel apiece.

In 1944, they were outgrowing their space and bought the Magnolia, a seafood restaurant on the corner of Circuit Avenue and Lake Street, across from the Flying Horses. The building extended across half the block with a garden area between the restaurant and the next building.

Edwardo ran the restaurant, and Maria ran the clam bar, one of the first on the Island. By this time their son Wilfred had married Antoinette, and both were working there as well. Their son, also Wilfred, whom

The Commonwealth of Massachusetts

Town of Oak Bluffs

Common Victualler's License

This is to Certify that the BOARD OF SELECTMEN hereby grants a COMMON VICTUALLER'S LICENSE to

Mary Jordan

at *Italian - American Restaurant*

Park Avenue

.... in said Town

until May 1, 19 33, and at that place only.

This license is issued in conformity with the authority granted to the Selectmen of Towns by Chapter 140 of the General Laws and amendments thereto, and expires on the thirtieth day of April, A. D. 19 33, unless sooner suspended or revoked for violation of the Laws of the Commonwealth respecting the licensing of Innholders or Common Victuallers.

This license is subject to the provisions of Chapter 140, General Laws 1921, and amendments thereto.

Witness our hands, this .... 18th .... day of *August* 1932.

Michael J. Ferguson
Norman L. Pratt
James H. Woodard

} Selectmen of Oak Bluffs.

To get their victualler's license, Maria Giordano signed the license as Mary Jordan. It worked! *Courtesy of Buster Giordano.*

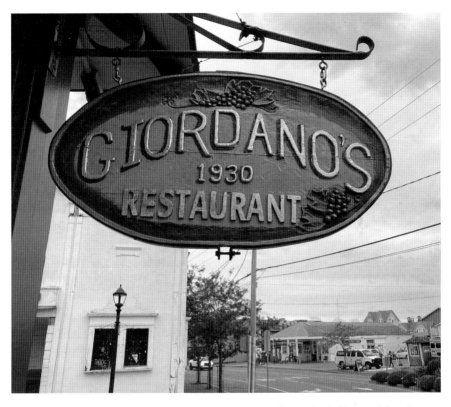

The Giordano's sign is a welcome announcement summer has arrived. *Courtesy of Joyce Dresser.*

we know today as Buster, accompanied his mother to work daily. She worked in the clam bar and placed infant Buster in a drawer beside her in the kitchen. There can be no argument that Buster was born into the restaurant business.

When Buster Giordano was old enough, he mopped the floor, moved on to peeling potatoes, worked in the clam bar, and finally moved to the main kitchen, which he still oversees today. Buster often tells the story of a wooden sink in one of their first buildings. It had a plug in the bottom and had to be filled with water daily until the wood expanded and held the water.

For years, Wilfred Sr. managed the book-keeping until the 1960s, when his son Buster introduced him to Valerie, a computer programmer. Valerie became the bookkeeper and still is today. She and Buster married, and the family tradition of working at Giordano's continued.

Chicken Special

**SOUTHERN FRIED CHICKEN
IN A BASKET**
With Chips
Hot Rolls and Butter
95c

Soups

Chicken Soup, plain or with Noodles, Rice or Greens	.30	Minestrone	.30
Clam Chowder	.40	Vegetable	.30
		Noodle	.30

Spaghetti

Spaghetti with Butter	.75	Spaghetti with Meat Sauce	.65
Spaghetti with Oil and Garlic	.75	Spaghetti with Meat Balls	.80
Spaghetti with Anchovies	.80	Spaghetti with Mushrooms	.90
Spaghetti with Little Necks	.90	Spaghetti with Calabrese Sauce	.80
Ravioli with Meat Sauce	.75	Spaghetti with Marinara Sauce	.75

Steaks and Chops

Broiled Pork Chops	1.25	Broiled Sirloin Steak	
Broiled Veal Chops	1.25	Broiled Tenderloin Steak	
Veal Cutlet with Tomato Sauce	.95	Sirloin Steak a la Pizzaiola	
Veal a la Cacciatore	1.25	Broiled Lamb Chops	
Veal Cutlet a la Calabrese	1.35	Broiled Chopped Sirloin	.95
Veal Steak a la Calabrese	1.50		

Served with French Fried Potatoes and Salad.

Seafood

Scallops a la Cacciatore	1.25	Broiled Chicken Lobster	1.75
Fried Scallops, Fr. Fr. Pot.	.95	Cold Lobster Plate, Fr. Fr. Pot.	1.75
Fried Clams, Fr. Fr. Pot.	.90	Lobster a la Cacciatore	2.00
Steamed Clams with Butter	.75	Fried Lobster, Fr. Fr. Pot.	1.75
Little Necks on half shell	.35		

Served with French Fried Potatoes and Salad.
Hot Rolls and Butter

Chicken

Half Fried Chicken	1.50	Chicken a la Cacciatore	1.75
Half Broiled Chicken	1.50	Chicken a la Calabrese	1.75

Served with French Fried Potatoes and Salad.

Massachusetts

The menu at Giordano's hasn't changed that much over the years. The same can't be said about the prices, however. *Courtesy of Buster Giordano.*

The restaurant used to open July 4 every year and close by Labor Day. As each generation retired, the next generation took over. Buster's generation currently oversees the restaurant, while his brother Richie runs the pizza room. Richie learned to throw a pizza in his teens, when his father hired Luigi, another Italian, who taught him.

Giordano family members continue to have a strong work ethic, as the restaurant is open seven days a week, all summer. The pizza room and clam bar open the first Thursday in May and stay open until Indigenous People's Day in October. The restaurant opens a little later and closes on Tivoli Day, the second Saturday in September. The day the pizza room and clam bar open has always been exciting. A story goes that a woman driving past saw they were open, stopped her car, and announced it on her CB scanner. People came in droves.

As fashion has changed over the years, so has people's taste in food. The open-faced turkey sandwiches and spaghetti with anchovies that were once popular have given way to pasta with a creamy pesto or alfredo sauce. Currently, the most popular dish is chicken Parmesan. For many years, at the end of the season Giordano's has offered a turkey dinner night. On such a night, they would serve one hundred pounds of turkey and sell out. On another night, they offered "pasta your way": you choose your pasta, sauce, vegetables, and protein. This was another sell-out night.

Buster and Valerie have four children all involved in the business. Billy, who studied restaurant and hotel management, runs the kitchen, and prepares a fresh soup daily; Jason studied business and runs the clam bar; Carl works in the kitchen preparing salads, appetizers, and his famous homemade pudding, which started with rice custard but has evolved into a candy bar–laced confection. Carl also studied computer graphic design and creates the menus and signs. Daughter Leanne is the restaurant manager.

Wilfred Giordano Jr. has always been known as Buster. He is the third generation of the venerable family to run the popular seasonal restaurant. *Courtesy of Joyce Dresser.*

Richie and Nancy's son Michael runs the pizza room with his dad, who began throwing pizza at fourteen. Members of the fifth generation are now showing their faces, with Ryan, Elana, and Eva working in the clam bar, waiting tables, bussing, or tending bar.

The only restriction the family has is no planning a summer wedding. Now we know why.

3. The Home Port Restaurant Oyster Bar, 1931

"Tasteful simplicity is the keynote in finishing and furnishing of this establishment, and there is always a breeze sweeping up from the water a stone's throw away." These pleasing words in the first advertisement of the Home Port set the tone for the tenure of the iconic restaurant.[85]

The Home Port is recognized for traditional and inspired seafood fare in the fishing port of Menemsha. The sunsets are unique on the East Coast: looking west to see the sun set into the ocean. The Home Port offers classic lobster dinners in the semi-rough, the original fried oyster, clam chowder, and the freshest of Menemsha seafood. Chilmark is dry but encourages guests to bring a bottle for a corking fee. As their motto says, "Leave the Shells, Take the Memories."[86]

In the early summer of 1931, Captain Chester Robinson and his wife opened a lunch counter in Menemsha Creek, Chilmark, to meet the wants and needs of local fishermen and the occasional tourist. Quahog chowder and a lobster roll met their customers' desires, and the Home Port came into existence, just as the Great Depression closed many businesses across the country.

The Home Port cycled through a few owners, but in 1945, Chet Sterns bought it and ran it for a dozen years. Then a third Chet and his wife, Esther (Rabbit) Cummens, purchased the Home Port in 1957, expanding the facility and the menu while eliminating lunch service. Chet Cummens improved the seasonal dinners and increased the prestige with the freshest seafood, large servings, and simple cooking. The Home Port evolved into an Island institution under Chet and Esther.

Enter Will Holtham in 1967. He spent a decade ascending the food ladder from mopping floors to working the stove. Will Holtham bought the Home

The original Home Port fed local fishermen and an occasional tourist venturing out to Menemsha in the 1930s. *Courtesy of the* Home Port Cookbook.

Port in 1977 and ran it thirty-something years. He endeared himself to the staff with his strong work ethic. He engaged celebrities from Jimmy Cagney to Paul Newman. And he was always on the lookout to improve his culinary offerings, expand his facility, and grow his business.

Will Holtham established the Home Port as a destination restaurant, drawing celebrities to its authentic seaside setting for delicious seafood.

In the 1980s, he opened The Bite, a clam bar down the street, but sold it to longtime employee Karen Flynn. The Bite closed in 2017.

When he sought to expand into the off-season, Holtham bought the Square Rigger, in Edgartown, and converted that lounge-restaurant into a thriving site for fine dining. He sold it when he realized he belonged at the Home Port.

In 2009, at the age of sixty, Will Holtham sold the Home Port to Bob and Sarah Nixon, who owned the nearby Beach Plum Inn. The Nixons ran the Home Port for a decade but failed to open for a couple of years due to staffing and Covid complications.

In the spring of 2022, the Home Port was purchased by Boston restaurateur Seth Woods, a seasonal Aquinnah resident, and Eric Berke. The new owners reopened for the 2022 season, and the Home Port continues its fine dining tradition beyond its ninetieth year.

Holtham's *Home Port Cookbook* (2011) has a host of recipes that verify his authenticity as a creative chef. With forewords by the likes of James Taylor and Michael J. Fox, the *Home Port Cookbook* is a delight to poke through. As Holtham noted in the frontispiece, "Cooking doesn't have to be a tedious, difficult, scary profession. Preparing dinner should be as enjoyable as eating it. It's as simple as that." Will Holtham passed in 2020 at the age of seventy-one.

4. The Kafe, 1933

"The Wharf Pub and Restaurant first opened its doors as The Edgartown Café, or just the Kafe as it was called, in 1933. Ralph Levinson of Edgartown started the restaurant. It was a favorite stop for Edgartown fishermen and yacht club sailors for years, a place where one could always get a good steak." Tony Omer added, "It is one of a few Edgartown restaurants that stays open all winter. It is an oasis in the desert of winter Edgartown."[87]

The Kafe had a huge dining room that stretched from lower Main Street across to Mayhew Lane. It proved popular with local fishermen and yacht club members over the years. Fans of the café dubbed it the Kafe, *the* place to get a good steak.

Another perspective on the Kafe was offered by Eekie Wolff of Edgartown: "There was so little to choose from back then." As a child, she lived across the street from the Kafe. "I could look out of my bedroom window and watch the drunks brawling. I had so much fun watching what was going on across the street."

One fan recalled the Kafe had a large dining room where people like Walter Cronkite enjoyed baked stuffed lobster, with an old fashioned.

Brion McGroarty recalled, "The Kafe was owned by a great guy named Ralph Levinson who owned the real estate." After the Kafe closed in August 1982, "the real estate was sold to Jim and Marjorie (Convery) Rankin. They did a total renovation and created The Wharf Restaurant and Wharf Pub. I purchased the restaurant business." Brion McGroarty and his family operated the Wharf from 1986 to 2004. Meredith Goldthwait waitressed at the Wharf when it transitioned from the Kafe to the Wharf.

In 2019, the McGroartys opened MV Wine and Spirits by the airport, a welcome site for thirsty Vineyarders that annually earns the Best of the Vineyard award. Sharing customers with the Fish House and Black Sheep creates an oasis for the up-Island population.

Today, the Wharf Pub and Restaurant is run by another family, the Coogans. Liza Coogan and her three children bought the restaurant in 2004, with Will Coogan as the restaurant manager. They enjoy hosting locals and tourists with local seafood, live music, and televised sporting events.

5. ArtCliff Diner, 1938

The ArtCliff reopened in the autumn of 2023 after a two-year renovation project. We had to reacquaint ourselves with this Island icon. We rounded up a couple of couples and headed for this café by Five Corners.

The diner aura permeates the space: retro atmosphere, familiar faces, fine food, fun feelings. You never know who you'll run into at the ArtCliff.

We spotted a foursome of actors at a nearby table finishing a last cup of coffee with the star of their show, Billy Baloo, aka Willy Mason. Joyce engaged Mil, Doug, and Lee as she enjoyed their capers at the Vineyard Playhouse. Hardscrabble gold miners, adorned in cowboy hats and suspenders, the trio sang and danced and performed a Greek chorus to Baloo's saga. It was a hoot!

We gravitated to our table for six and savored the atmosphere. The menu options of tasty breakfast dishes are mouthwatering. The walls are adorned with artwork; a shelf of tchotchke recalls an earlier era, vivid reminders of the ArtCliff's storied past.

The saga of the ArtCliff reads like a Greek myth. In the 1930s, a rundown Worcester Lunch Car Company diner sat across from the current Oak Bluffs police station. Twenty-two-year-old Ralph Brown convinced his father, St. Clair Brown, to co-sign the $800 loan to purchase the car and move it to Edgartown. Ralph's partner, his brother-in-law Howard Nickerson, said, "I'll be the only man in history who has ridden from Oak Bluffs to Edgartown in a diner." And he was. The steel wheels of the diner made quite a racket. The young men planted the dining car in the parking lot off lower Main Street, by the Yacht Club.

Captain Brown's Galley opened in April 1938. It featured a nautical theme, with a novice waiter at the counter and a novice cook on the grill.

A group of hungry customers appreciates the cuisine and ambiance afforded every ArtCliff guest. *Courtesy of Joyce Dresser.*

Ralph and Nick made a go of it that summer, open twenty-four hours, seven days a week. They kept at it the following summers. In 1941, they bought a second diner in Keene, New Hampshire, followed by a third in Concord two years later. "Worcester Lunch Car diners were well known for the high quality of the work, and handcrafted wooden elements. The diners were noteworthy because of the monitor roof with clerestory windows to allow ventilation of cooking odors."[88] Ralph and Nick were ready to move on.

They sold Captain Brown's Galley to Art Silva and Cliff Luce in 1943. The new owners moved the diner from Edgartown to Vineyard Haven. "From then on, the ArtCliff has been a home away from home for Island visitors and locals, serving food with a side of Vineyard history, a friendly attitude and unique vintage décor," as the placemat proclaims.

Oak Bluffs to Edgartown, then Vineyard Haven—the ArtCliff finally settled on its current site. Curiously, records of the Worcester Lunch Car Company indicate in 1947 a new diner, #824, was shipped to Vineyard Haven, adding to the ArtCliff's mythical genesis.

The diner was replaced by a new structure in 1963.[89]

Plans were sent out for bid by Arthur Silva. (Art and Cliff Luce were still on scene.) "The plans call for a single-story structure of modern design, the front chiefly of glass." There's more: "The interior arrangement is to be similar to that of the present restaurant, in that it will have lunch-bar and tables in different areas."[90]

This tiny article inspired a lengthy letter from Shirley Anthony, who was "distressed to read in the paper today about the proposed building going up in place of the ArtCliff Diner." She asked, rhetorically, "Why does the new structure have to be a modern building, boasting of glass, square and homely? Why can't it be like the buildings they put up in Edgartown?"

Anthony worried that "the little harbor town of Vineyard Haven will gradually resemble any commercial area along the main Cape Cod roads." She preferred structures "along the lines of old Cape Cod styling and architecture; weathered shingles and the like."

The ArtCliff transitioned from an old railroad car diner into a modern facility, circa 1963.

While turkey is still on the menu, the prices are higher than in 1943. *Courtesy of Joyce Dresser.*

"The poor Art Cliff," wrote Susie Middleton in 2000. "Since Art Silva and Cliff Luce—the original owners who moved the former Captain Brown Diner from Edgartown to Vineyard Haven in 1943—had sold the business, the diner had suffered from decay and debt."

When she first arrived on the Vineyard in 2000, Gina Stanley was not impressed. "I pulled up to the diner and it was in tough shape. The diner had been closed down, but there were dirty dishes in the kitchen and the ceiling was leaking."

Yet Gina is still behind the counter, years later. And the ArtCliff has been reborn in its recent incarnation, with an office and storage space upstairs.

Gina Stanley arrived on Martha's Vineyard with a dream and a workaholic attitude, essential for her profit margin. She honed her talents in front of the stove and the front of the house, as Susie Middleton put it. Graduating from the Culinary Institute of America in 1991, Gina transitioned from Washington's five-star St. Regis Hotel to pastry chef at Blair House, the president's guest house for foreign heads of state. Blair House held Gina a couple years, but she wanted more. An ad for the ArtCliff in 2000 piqued her curiosity, and she's still here, after two decades and counting.

"If you see lines out a restaurant's front door and around to the back," wrote Lisa Belcastro in *Vineyard Style*, "and people talking and waiting in the parking lot for over an hour for a meal, you can bet the place is worth the wait. The ArtCliff Diner is such a place." Frequented by locals and tourists alike, the ArtCliff is very much alive and flourishing after all these years. Serving traditionally good food is a skill that deserves a return visit.

And the atmosphere "is warm and inviting without the slightest bit of pretention, and the cozy 48-seat room feels a bit as though you're sitting down to a large family meal, with or without your family."

"Personally, I'm happy at any table with one of Gina's frittatas," admitted Belcastro, a frequent customer, writer, and runner of marathons. "Yukon gold potatoes, scrambled eggs and a variety of add-ins that make breakfast the best meal of the day."[91]

Austin Racine, who knows his way around a kitchen, assisted Gina Stanley when she needed it. His calm manner and expertise as a chef proved a perfect match for the ArtCliff. Today Austin runs Mo's Kitchen at the PA Club, catching the noontime crowd who know a good sandwich when they eat it.

When Art Silva and Cliff Luce opened the Diner, the men had a round table where friends gathered. The Round Table became an institution passed down through the generations.

Gina says, "We still have the Round Table. I don't want the boys mad at me!"

Denys Wortman is one of many Islanders who came of age at the ArtCliff. In his high school yearbook of 1957, he noted: Diner Club 1, 2, 3, 4. Denny knew Art and Cliff; Ann Silva was in his high school class, as was Cliff's son. He added, "It's a place you can call home. Home, with nice people and great food. Doesn't get any better than that."

Gina holds true to the original diner, although the prices are slightly higher than those circa 1943. "I've always loved history and vintage things. The diner fuels my passion. I wasn't looking to change it. I wanted it to be what it was."[92]

Middleton continued, "And those are her fans waiting outside the diner. Islanders, visitors, celebs, politicians—they're all in line. With the ArtCliff, Gina has achieved something unique—a down-home vibe that also feels hip, with food that can satisfy everyone from a picky child to a serious foodie."

Gina has expanded the range of the ArtCliff, offering catering services, a food truck, and donations to local nonprofits like Camp Jabberwocky and the Boys and Girls Club. During the pandemic, "we pivoted overnight to take-out and food by what you could pay or free." She added, "People were very generous in leaving money to cover the free meals."

"There's so much history," Gina reminded Susie Middleton. "It's funny, but I never really felt like the diner was mine. I've always felt like I was taking care of it for someone else, keeping it going to pass along to the next caretaker."[93]

Connie Berry reviewed the culinary delights at the ArtCliff: "I raved about the Vineyard Cobb Salad, with all its myriad of ingredients. She said she didn't want to put a traditional Cobb salad on the menu, and she had a pretty good idea that all the ingredients would go together. 'The egg on top is more of a European thing,' Gina told me."

She continued, "It's all pretty basic, but I really try to keep it up to date with what people are asking for: Atkins, to gluten-free, to vegetarian to Vegan. Tastes have changed in 23 years.

"It's very fast-paced, so there is a lot of room for error. I do my best, rely on the workers to also want to make everyone's experience special. I know this is some folks' highlight of the day. We owe it to them to do our best!"

Connie continued her culinary critique: "Maybe she dreams of menu selections like Hen's on Deck (grilled chicken, mozzarella, tomato, basil mayo, and arugula on ciabatta), and jots them down in the middle of the night. Once I spoke with Gina, who's cooked and done everything else at the ArtCliff for years, it all made sense."[94] The ArtCliff is one-of-a-kind, thanks to Gina Stanley and her legion of great employees and enthusiastic fans.

6. Humphrey's, 1941

Argie Humphrey managed the Farmers Market in West Tisbury through the Depression years to the onset of World War II. With sugar rationing, he closed the market and, in 1941, opened the Vineyard Foodshop in Vineyard Haven. Later he built a new bakery/shop by his house in North Tisbury, at the intersection of State and North Roads, across from the lone oak.

Ann Lees of Chilmark and Brookline offered a memory: "There is a wonderful story waiting for you about Humphrey's Bakery in North Tisbury. When we first came to the Vineyard in the mid-1970s, it was a destination culinary stop. It was owned and run by Argie Humphrey. They had the best jelly donuts and Portuguese sweet bread you ever ate."

As a child, Alice Early's family would stop at Humphrey's after church for butterscotch cookies with crushed butterscotch pieces in each cookie. "They were so crunchy!" she recalled. "A real treat."

Today, Life at Humphrey's continues that original business in Woodland Center on State Road in Vineyard Haven. (True confessions: it is run by our son-in-law Pete Smyth, former owner of Slice of Life in Oak Bluffs and Humphrey descendant Donna Diaz.)

Laura Holmes Haddad alerted readers to a short-lived special fall treat: apple cider donuts. Whether it's because of the cooler evenings, shorter days, or colorful autumn leaves, apple cider donuts appear in bakeshops across New England. Perhaps because of the preponderance of apples, the apple cider donut is a favorite across New England.

Her explanation fills in the details. Only in the fall, and only on Saturday mornings, Pete Smyth of Life at Humphrey's makes apple cider donuts to order. It is *the* place to go for these fleeting treats.

Right: The best apple cider donuts on Martha's Vineyard are baked at Life at Humphrey's in Vineyard Haven. *Courtesy of Joyce Dresser.*

Below: Pete Smyth was the owner/chef at Slice of Life for fifteen years. Today, with Donna Diaz, he runs Life at Humphrey's, a popular sandwich bakery. *Courtesy of Joyce Dresser.*

Alex Schwartz, the Apple Cider Donuteur, determines the premier apple cider donut in various locales. Pete Smyth's apple cider donut at Life at Humphrey's is the only donut in all of Martha's Vineyard to make the Cider Donut map of New England.

"This seasonal flavor dates back to the first American settlers, who used leftover fat from the autumn hog slaughter to fry dough into the circular donut we know today. With warm fall spices like nutmeg and cinnamon joining the tang of fresh apple cider, the apple cider donut is a classic for a reason."[95]

Haddad explained, "Life at Humphrey's co-owner and baker Peter Smyth has a brand-new fryer and makes his classic cake-based apple cider donuts late September through November." Acidity in cider makes the donuts tender. Pete serves them hot, bathed in cinnamon sugar, only Saturday mornings.

7. Aquinnah Shop Restaurant, 1948

In the 1940s, Wampanoag Tribal Chief Napoleon Madison ran a food stand at the Gay Head Cliffs, selling hot dogs, hamburgers, and Coke. One side of his gas grill kept the coffee hot, while he cooked on the other side.

Tour buses or taxis brought tourists from down-Island who frequented Napoleon Madison's stand. Anne Vanderhoop, Juli's mother, baked cookies there. The more she worked, the larger her role became. Anne began baking pies. By 1948, the business had morphed into the Aquinnah Shop Restaurant.

From the late 1940s to 2016, Anne Vanderhoop and her family ran the Aquinnah Shop Restaurant. It was the premier dining site on the Cliffs, with a gorgeous view of the southwest corner of Martha's Vineyard across to Jamestown, Rhode Island. The food, prepared right on the premises, met the needs of a hungry tourist population.

However, in 2016, the Aquinnah Shop was sold out of the Wampanoag tribe. In 2023, it was sold to the Aquinnah Land Initiative but held by the Native Land Conservancy until ALI raised the $2 million purchase price.

Wenonah Madison Sauer, great-granddaughter of Napoleon and Nanette Madison, is president of the Aquinnah Land Initiative, with an all-female Wampanoag Board of Directors. Wenonah takes special pride in tribal women who have protected ancestral properties.

Wenonah is pleased the Aquinnah Shop is once again under the jurisdiction of the Wampanoag tribe. She said ALI recognizes "the cultural understanding that our bodies are not separate from our land." Its mission is to restore "the sacred relationship between native people and our ancestral lands." The Aquinnah Land Initiative ensures the Aquinnah Shop will once more become a Wampanoag-owned operation.[96]

One local contributor summed up the situation with the Aquinnah Shop Restaurant:

Let's not forget it was the old-timers who worked and kept this restaurant open from Easter through October, and then had the best party. Thanks to Luther and Anne working twelve hours plus, seven days a week. Without them, it could never have happened. The Madison and Vanderhoop families and generations of their earthly family worked it (three generations of mine). Napoleon Madison started it with his son continuing, not the tribe, though honorable members. The land was always separate from the other cliffs shops. Sadly, no one can replace Anne and Luther.[97]

And the latest word, in the winter of 2024, is that the Aquinnah Shop Restaurant will open in the summer of 2024. Wenonah Madison was quoted as saying, "There are plans to open this season, but they're still being ironed out."[98] The Shop will operate under new management with a Wampanoag-owned business leasing the facility. It will be the talk of the town for this landmark restaurant to be open once more.

8. Menemsha Galley, 1950

The Menemsha Galley sits on the edge of Menemsha basin, a sunset site for locals and tourists alike. With a porch almost in the harbor, the location rivals the culinary delights on the menu. The Galley opened in 1950 and built a reputation for fries, salads, burgers, clam chowder, lobster rolls, and soft-serve ice cream.

In 1999, siblings Barbara and Frank Fenner and Frank's wife, Merrily, took over the Galley. Barbara manned the kitchen with her specialties: clam chowder, crab cakes, and white bean vegetarian sandwiches, to name a few.

In 2018, the Fenner family sold the Menemsha Galley to Tony Saccoccia, who ran The Feast of Chilmark in the '80s and '90s and more recently was chef at The Grill on Main. Jack O'Malley, chef instructor of the culinary arts department at the high school, joined him in running the Galley.

The Menemsha Galley continues a tradition of seventy-five years of filling the bellies and warming the hearts of locals and visitors to Menemsha.

9. Scottish Bakehouse, 1961

It was in 1961, the first year of the Kennedy administration, that Isabella Maxwell White departed her native land of Pebbleshire, Scotland, for Martha's Vineyard. As the website of the eponymous Scottish Bakehouse reports, "She won the hearts of Islanders not only with her shortbread and kidney pies, but also with her sense of humor, Yorkshire terriers, and her tradition of making holiday meals for the home-bound elderly on Thanksgiving, Christmas, and Easter."

Many young Islanders worked for Mrs. White over her three and a half decades running the Bakehouse. When she passed in 1997, her three children—Peter, Isabel, and Robert—continued to run the Bakehouse for several years.

In 2004, Daniele Barrick assumed ownership of the Scottish Bakehouse, having acquired culinary experience and expertise at the ArtCliff Diner. Daniele was intrigued with homemade cooking, learning under the auspices of her Italian grandmother.

10. Square Rigger, 1963

The Square Rigger opened as a restaurant in 1963, but its structure has a more complicated past. Allegedly built near Edgartown Great Pond by a whaling captain, Thomas Pease, about 1800, the house was moved in 1949 to the Edgartown Triangle by Manuel Duarte. The house went through numerous ownership changes before it was purchased in 1963 and John Donnelly opened it as a restaurant.

When Will Holtham of the Home Port in Menemsha bought the Rigger in 1984 from the estate of John Donnelly, he referred to it as a lounge, rather than a restaurant, in his *Home Port Cookbook*. However, the Square Rigger was open year-round, and Holtham felt he could make a go of it in the off-season. He expanded the menu, which had only a half-dozen entrees, "but they were all fantastic," Holtham wrote. He added an open hearth and increased menu options with bouillabaisse, steak, and chops.

By 1994, Holtham recognized the Rigger had met his goals of a larger menu, a year-round clientele, and a great staff, headed by Tony and Doreen Rezendes. As Geoff Currier reported, "It was Dec. 31, 1994." Tony said: "I'll never forget that day. Will said to us, 'You folks have worked hard, it's time you owned the place. You can buy the business and lease the real estate— the only money I want is enough to cover my mortgage.'" The Rezendeses assumed ownership of the Square Rigger, with their son Dana the sous chef and daughters Amy and Jenny as waitresses. Tony cooked. "So Tony and Dana were working in the kitchen, Amy and Jenny were waitressing, and I was managing the restaurant—this was truly a family business," Doreen said. The Rezendeses expanded the menu to nearly forty entrées, cooking lobster eight different ways, adding clams casino, prime rib, and baked stuffed shrimp.

Tony Rezendes passed in December 2023 at eighty-one. It was noted in his obituary he was "born with the gift of gab," and his greatest success was running the Square Rigger. "Through this iconic Island eatery he could humbly share the talents of his family for years. Tony answered the phone, baked perfect popovers and tirelessly cooked large batches of scratch-made quahog chowder." Under Tony Rezendes, the Rigger radiated with stories and fables, history, and camaraderie, and for many diners, eating there served as a rite of passage.

Geoff Currier noted, "The Square Rigger catered to a healthy blend of seasonal and year-round clientele whom the Rezendeses look on as extended family." As the pandemic impacted Island businesses, the Rigger had developed an expansive takeout opportunity, so the transition worked well, from the dining room to the takeout window.

Then, in December 2022, the *Vineyard Gazette* reported, "The Square Rigger—a longtime staple for everything from fried seafood to chowder to cheeseburgers—has come under new ownership."

Owner Jenny Dowd, the daughter of Tony and Doreen Rezendes, informed selectmen that the restaurant would be under new management yet still known as the Square Rigger. "She thanked patrons and staff for 27 years of management," and wrote, "We will be forever grateful to all those who were a special part of our journey."[99]

The new owners are Nina's Incorporated, under Chef Sandro Silvio, serving Brazilian specialties.[100]

11. Black Dog, 1971

In the first edition of *The Black Dog: Summer on the Vineyard* cookbook, editor Joe Hall credited Charlie Esposito for working more than a quarter century at the Black Dog, both in the kitchen and on the floor, or the front of the house. Charlie is a living legend at the Black Dog.

We sat down over breakfast with Charlie to ask about his tenure at the Black Dog.

In the early 1970s, Charlie Esposito arrived on Martha's Vineyard to perform with his band and pursue his artwork. By 1975, he was working at the Black Dog in Vineyard Haven, mopping floors. He quickly rose up the food chain. Before long, he was washing dishes, which led to bussing and finally taking full charge of the floor. In the early days of the Black Dog, the atmosphere was one of "let's play restaurant." At that time, the daily menu was etched on a blackboard. There was no standardized menu, as dishes were prepared with the latest fresh ingredients.

Charlie shared the backstory of how the Black Dog Restaurant was born.

Robert Douglas and Allan Miller were eating at the Artcliff Diner one day when Douglas mentioned he had some land on the harbor. And he was purchasing materials from off-island. In the deal he made, he had to take everything. Everything included some huge beams. Those huge beams were used in the construction of the restaurant Allan Miller built. The interior of the Black Dog was recycled nineteenth-century yellow pine. The size of the building was determined by how long the beams were and how many there were. The open kitchen is in the same location, facing Vineyard Haven Harbor, as when it was built in 1971. Allan Miller, the master builder, became the first manager. The current manager is Rob Douglas, one of Bob's four sons.

Jeff Livingston, who lived on Chappaquiddick, was one of the first chefs. He would bring fresh fish to the Black Dog to add to the menu. In the early days, Sally Knight made chowder at her house and then put the pot of soup on the front seat of her car and drove to the restaurant. Breakfast dishes were devised and named for various reasons, as they are today. One kitchen worker liked the cartoon *Scooby Doo*, so that became the name of an egg dish. Another dish was named for Loretta Balla, owner of the Seaview Hotel in Oak Bluffs. Happy Jeff is a breakfast dish named for stalwart breakfast chef Jeff Heflin. Jeff's wife, Amy, works alongside him as a waitress.

When winters were slow in the 1970s and '80s, the restaurant began to offer ethnic nights. Monday was Greek night, featuring the gourmet food and belly-dancing of Helios Restaurant; Tuesdays were Italian nights, orchestrated by Christina Napolitano, who prepared 150 dinners. Wednesdays were Mexican; Thursday nights were Chinese nights. Because Charlie Esposito was proficient at Chinese cooking, he prepared meals for Chinese night. Every week, he went to Chinatown in Boston to get ingredients for the two hundred dinners he would prepare that night. As time went by, co-workers joined him for the trip, which made it more of a party atmosphere. His special lo mein dish cost about $12.95.

At that time, there was a jukebox in the dining room. People lived upstairs, which is now an office. The staff's uniform included a T-shirt with a black dog on it. When customers began requesting to buy a Black Dog T-shirt, Elaine Miller realized this was a great marketing opportunity. Today, the ubiquitous Black Dog T-shirt is world-famous.

Two men were daily customers. They commandeered the table in front of the fireplace for breakfast and lunch. The two were Ed Warsyk and Don Clinton. Every day, Ed would ask for a menu, look it over, and

Charlie Esposito cooked at the Black Dog for decades. He honored Ed Warsyk, a Black Dog customer for twenty-five years. *Courtesy of Joyce Dresser.*

order a BLT. To honor him, Charlie sculpted a bronze sandwich on a plate with a cup of coffee. Today it is on display in the restaurant with a plaque honoring Ed.

Charlie worked at the restaurant for thirty years. As teenagers, his children worked alongside him, Echo as a cashier, while Anthony and Augusto "Augie" bussed. After Charlie left the kitchen, he was recruited to help with the technological needs of the Black Dog. When Charlie retired

The welcome sign at the Black Dog features a black lab, reminiscent of the dog in *Treasure Island*. The Black Dog restaurant is an Island treasure. *Courtesy of Joyce Dresser.*

from the Black Dog, he became a private chef and returned to his studio, where he recorded Vineyard Sound, Johnny Hoy, and Entrain, among others. He has done voiceovers for Walter Cronkite and Mike Wallace.

Today, Charlie is employed by the high school Performing Arts Center; his son Anthony has taken over his studio.

12. Linda Jean's, 1976

Linda Jean's approaches its fiftieth year of operation in 2026.

Linda Jean's reopened in early 2023 under the management of "Lisa and Winston Christie, who are the owners of the well-received spot Winston's Kitchen, which gained a great reputation for its dynamite sandwiches. This news quickly made Linda Jean's something to look forward to."[101]

Marc Hanover opened Linda Jean's in 1976 and ran it for forty-seven years. He made it *the* year-round go-to restaurant in Oak Bluffs for decades. Since he retired, he realizes how much he misses the staff and customers he's known for ages. He plans to help Winston as a consultant in the summer.

"Not many restaurants have been run by the same owner for forty-seven years!" Hanover noted. Now he enjoys sleeping later in the morning and spending time with his grandchildren. It was a good run. And he's happy to see Linda Jean's continue to thrive.

The Christies knew they were taking on a promising project when they agreed to operate the facility on Circuit Avenue. Known for the bottomless cup of coffee, fresh luncheon plates, and delectable dinner options, Linda Jean's reputation was too enticing to turn down.

We chatted with Winston, who proved his prowess with the success of Winston's Take-Out on the Oak Bluffs Harbor, next to Our Market, which opened in 2022. What made you think Winston's would succeed? "We found the space and converted it to a take-out," Winston said. "Quality, consistency, and a good menu." The fried chicken sandwiches and dinners are the most popular, although the steak and cheese sandwich and oxtail dinner run close.

Winston Christie trained under Chef David Joyce of Chesca's, who, in turn, graduated from the Culinary Institute of America. Winston learned the trade, one step removed from the academic institute, and put in time at Back Door Donuts and Murdick's Fudge.

The biggest problem in managing two eateries? In a word, *staffing*. Winston and Lisa share the responsibilities of scheduling people to work, giving them time off for family or appointments as well as days off. There's a lot of staff interaction between the two facilities, less than a half mile apart, both serving breakfast, lunch, and dinner.

What improvements have you made at LJ's? "They had a liquor license, but we added a bar," he said. With drinks like Caribbean Mule, Winston's Old Fashioned, and the Nutty Jamaican, who wouldn't want to sample a cocktail? Or two?

Linda Jean's most popular dinner dish? Winston thought a moment before he named the turkey dinner.

In 2022, Winston and Lisa Christie opened Winston's popular take-out shop on the Oak Bluffs Harbor. In 2023, they became managers of Linda Jean's, a half-mile away. *Courtesy of Joyce Dresser.*

That is the best meal in the house, although chicken Cordon Bleu, baked stuffed shrimp, and shrimp scampi entice a lot of diners.

Winston Christie thrives on being busy. He loves the challenge of running two food establishments simultaneously. He shows how excited he is, waving his arms at the opportunities, as well as the challenges of keeping everything running smoothly. What happens when you're over-tired, exhausted, stressed out? "I exercise. I dream up new specials to try." He smiles because he knows he's in the right place to get the job done.

And what would you like to see over the next ten years? "Four more Winston's!" he laughs. He would love to expand the takeout business but is very happy with just one Linda Jean's.

Lisa and Winston Christie have found the best ways to show their stuff.[102]

A few more popular restaurants sought inclusion in our top dozen eateries.

Coop de Ville opened in 1984 under Jeff Casara of Buffalo, selling chicken wings. In 1986, Carroll "Petey" Berndt of Baltimore bought the Coop, adding a raw bar and Baltimore specialties. The Coop prides itself on hosting World Cup soccer, always drawing a crowd. With a steady staff and loyal patrons, the Coop does all right. Steve Davidian of Dockside Jewelers favors the Coop.

The Coop is the first restaurant on Dockside to open for the season and last to close. Stocking one hundred beer varieties, myriad seafood dishes, and a spectacular sunset site, the Coop holds its own in the challenging restaurant trade. It has been a fixture overlooking Oak Bluffs Harbor for forty years.

Dock Street Coffee Shop sits right on Edgartown harbor. This greasy spoon, tucked in a hole in the wall, does a thriving year-round business with locals and tourists. It's a simple counter with stools, making it awkward for more than a couple of people in a party to converse. Yet the food is cooked right on the grill in front of you; the waitstaff is ready to meet your every need, and the ambiance is what you might expect: humble and practical, nothing fancy or pretentious. That's Dock Street.

"Opened in 1975, like many other vintage diners, Dock Street is no vestige, but a thriving eatery that has consistently served its regulars breakfast and lunch for many years. I felt at one in a place I knew…knew I could order eggs, bacon, and homefries. But that's the magic of diners and the magic of Dock Street. If you're looking for a place to eat, when you're feeling down and maybe beat, head to Dock Street, and take a seat. For what is finer than a diner."[103]

Woodland Grill is "the opposite of a tourist trap; if I go in there, I almost always see one of my old friends." The Grill offers a friendly atmosphere where everyone feels welcome.

"I think it's the simplicity and quality of the food and other odds and ends that Islanders seem to enjoy most. Hungry patrons aren't confronted with overcomplicated menus that seem to push the envelope of creativity a little too far."[104]

Nearly two decades earlier, Rob Baker was behind the grill, keeping everything under control.[105]

Rob has been slinging hash, so to speak, for more than twenty years and still is master of the establishment, remembering each diner's favorite sandwich, keeping the food coming, and making everyone feel happy about being there. It's a welcoming community at Woodland Grill.

7a foods has been a mainstay for up-Islanders since Daniel and Wenonah Madison Sauer opened in 2010. Tucked behind Alley's, in the heart of "downtown" West Tisbury, the sandwich shop offers a seasonal menu of tasty treats, soups, salads, frittatas, and baked goods. With a focus on fresh, farm food, Wenonah and Dan offer the mid-Island population a much-appreciated fast, friendly food service.

Looking ahead, we recognize recently opened restaurants already at the top of their game, voted Best New Restaurant of the year by voters in the *Martha's Vineyard Magazine* annual survey.

In 2021, Salvatore's Ristorante opened on Union Street, Vineyard Haven. As the magazine noted, "Salvatore della Torre opened his namesake restaurant in Vineyard Haven just when the Island needed some extra amore."

In 2022, Mo's Lunch, under Austin Racine and Maura Martin, was deemed a "gem of a restaurant inside the PA Club." The runner-up that year was Winston's, which offers "Great Food at Great Prices."

And in 2023, Bombay Indian Cuisine opened in Oak Bluffs across from Tony's Market, serving a wide variety of delicious Indian fare. "Folks can spice up their evenings with flavorful curries, such as vindaloo or rogan josh, and a side of warm naan."

As we ease along in the 2020s, this is what the future looks like.

In the mid-'90s, early in our relationship, I was impressed when Joyce whipped up a casserole, put it in an aluminum pan, covered it, and said she was taking it to a fellow teacher who was home sick. That gave me a good taste of life on the Vineyard.

EPILOGUE

*I*n writing the culinary history, we found fabric to create a patchwork of the Vineyard dining story.

Martha's Vineyard represents a miniature melting pot of America. In the beginning, Native Americans were the only humans on Island, hunting and gathering their food. When the white man came from England, he brought his taverns, his dining habits, and his cooking capabilities.

Native Vineyarders harvest shellfish and fish from the ocean, hunt deer, and forage the landscape. Farming expanded the Native American domain. Whaling ships brought Azoreans to our shores, along with their diet. Blacks introduced southern cooking. Immigrants from Europe came with Scottish haggis and Irish roasts. And Italian pastas. Today we are blessed with restaurants serving Asian, Caribbean, and Brazilian dishes.

Sharing cultures, menus, and customs, Vineyarders, and their visitors, have many choices. That is the melting pot, where many cultures overlap and share their dishes with the Island at large.

While we recognize the abundance of dining options, we acknowledge food insecurity among us. Martha's Vineyard has the image of an enclave for the rich and famous. The reality is middle-class households struggle to stretch a paycheck from one week to the next. Food insecurity is a reality.

Tom read *Stone Soup* to his first graders back in 1980 and recalls the folk tale with a moral. A stranger comes into town, where the people are hungry and selfish. No one is willing to share; it's every man for himself. The stranger starts to make soup, using only water and a stone. People gather round, curious. Townspeople are invited to add ingredients to make the broth taste better than just a rock in boiling water.

As neighbors add their vegetables and meat to the boiling cauldron, the soup takes shape. The denouement is that the medley of donations blend to be tastier and heartier than the vegetables alone.

The moral of sharing is appreciated by first graders. Adults should follow their lead.

And they are. The Vineyard is addressing food insecurity. When the Venezuelan migrants were dropped off in 2022, they were served soup. On Thanksgiving, Chef Deon cooks dozens of turkeys and myriad vegetables to provide meals for anyone and everyone.

Meals on Wheels, emanating from the Martha's Vineyard Hospital kitchen, are delivered year-round. Church suppers provide sustenance in winter months. Gleaning produce is shared at senior centers. West Tisbury and Oak Bluffs libraries offer free food. The Food Pantry has expanded in response to increased need. People on Martha's Vineyard are responding to food insecurity.

Our culinary history meandered along the shores, fields, and farms of Martha's Vineyard, harvesting local fish, meat, and produce. We savored fine dining from Salvatore's to State Road. The Little House in Vineyard Haven deserves a shout-out. We appreciate options from Mikado's Asian fare to a slice of Gio's pizza. From Humphrey's to 7 a, the Vineyard has a place at the table for everyone.

We enjoy a panoply of options, with an intriguing history, that shores up our current food system.

NOTES

Prologue

1. Brooke Kushwaha, "Vineyard History Is Food for Thought," *Vineyard Gazette*, June 5, 2023, https://vineyardgazette.com/news/2023/06/05/vineyard-history-food-thought.
2. Ibid.

Chapter 1

3. Diamond, *Guns, Grains, and Steel*, 107.
4. Ibid., 103.
5. King and Wexler, *Martha's Vineyard Cook Book*, xi.
6. Diamond, *Guns, Grains, and Steel*, 106.
7. Harris, *High on the Hog*, 44.
8. National Agricultural Library, www.nal.usda.gov.
9. Diamond, *Guns, Grains, and Steel*, 151.
10. Mollie Doyle, "The Three Sisters Sing: A Recipe from a Decolonized Diet," *Edible Vineyard*, October 15, 2021, https://ediblevineyard.com/2021/10/15/the-three-sisters-sing-a-recipe-from-a-decolonized-diet/.

Chapter 2

11. Joan Boyken, April 25, 2023.
12. Suzan Bellincampi, "A Bibulous Name," *Vineyard Gazette*, December 15, 2023.
13. King and Wexler, *Martha's Vineyard Cook Book*, 280.
14. Ibid., 289.
15. Ibid., 285–86.
16. Ibid., 273–75.

Chapter 3

17. *Gazette Chronicle*, October 7, 1966, reprinted in the *Vineyard Gazette*, October 6, 2023.
18. King and Wexler, *Martha's Vineyard Cook Book*, 33.
19. Dresser, *Martha's Vineyard in the American Revolution*, 110.

Chapter 5

20. Harris, *High on the Hog*, 82.
21. Dresser, *African Americans of Martha's Vineyard*, 73.
22. Harris, *My Soul*, 243.
23. Harris, *High on the Hog*.
24. Heather Hamacek, "Meals on Wheels Delivers; But Not Without Drivers," *Vineyard Gazette*, October 1, 2015, https://vineyardgazette.com/news/2015/10/01/meals-wheels-delivers-not-without-drivers#:~:text=In%20the%20past%20five%20years%2C%20the%20number%20of,on%20Wheels%3B%20the%20number%20is%20higher%20in%20summer.

Chapter 7

25. Ava Castro, "Harvest of the Month: Salad Greens," *MV Times*, June 23, 2021, https://www.mvtimes.com/2021/06/23/harvest-month-salad-greens/.
26. King and Wexler, *Martha's Vineyard Cook Book*, 5.
27. Welcome to Martha's Vineyard, https://mvol.com/marthas-vineyard-island-corn-right-right-now/.

28. Amy Traverso, "How to Make Beach Plum Jam," *New England*, July 2, 2022, https://newengland.com/food/condiments/beach-plum-jam-2/.
29. Christine Schultz, "O' Bluefish, Where Art Thou?," https://mvmagazine.com/news/2005/05/01/o-bluefish-where-art-thou.
30. *The Martha's Vineyard Cook Book* introduction.

Chapter 8

31. Mark Alan Lovewell, "Vineyard-Cape Commute: Crows Are Above It All," *Vineyard Gazette*, February 16, 2012, https://vineyardgazette.com/news/2012/02/16/vineyard-cape-commute-crows-are-above-it-all#:~:text=They%20all%20fly.%20The%20commuters%20are%20crows.%20They,around%204%20p.m.%20to%20spend%20the%20night%20here.
32. Lee, *Edible Wild Plants*, 6.
33. *Edible Vineyard*, Early Summer 2010.
34. *Vineyard Gazette*, February 15, 2024.

Chapter 9

35. *Vineyard Gazette*, July 3, 1936.
36. *Vineyard Gazette*, June 8, 2023.
37. *Vineyard Gazette*, July 9, 1974.
38. Teena Parton email on August 11, 2023.
39. *Martha's Vineyard Magazine*, October 2023.

Chapter 10

40. Mollie Doyle, "Home Sweet Home?" *Edible Vineyard*, May 13, 2022, https://ediblevineyard.com/2022/05/13/home-sweet-home/.
41. Julia Rappaport, "Young Restaurateurs Open with Moxie," *Vineyard Gazette*, May 22, 2008, https://vineyardgazette.com/news/2008/05/22/young-restaurateurs-open-moxie.
42. Julia Wells, "Musical Memories: David Crohan Marks 40 Years with Tabernacle," *Vineyard Gazette*, July 21, 2005, https://vineyardgazette.com/news/2005/07/21/musical-memories-david-crohan-marks-40-years-tabernacle.

43. Dresser, *Travel History of Martha's Vineyard*, 58.

44. *Vineyard Gazette*, November 17, 2023.

45. Phyllis Meras, "From Here to There and Helios, Lucia Moffett Charted a Fine Life," *Vineyard Gazette*, November 5, 2015, https://vineyardgazette.com/obituaries/2015/11/05/here-there-and-helios-lucia-moffett-charted-fine-life.

46. June Manning, "Helen Vanderhoop Manning Was Historian of Wampanoags," *Vineyard Gazette*, January 31, 2008, https://vineyardgazette.com/obituaries/2008/01/31/helen-vanderhoop-manning-was-historian-wampanoags.

47. Kaylea Moore, "A Peek into the Past: Martha's Vineyard Restaurants from Years Gone By," *MV Times*, March 13, 2013, https://www.mvtimes.com/2013/03/13/peek-into-past-marthas-vineyard-restaurants-from-years-gone-by-14700/.

48. Lee, *Vineyard Voices*, 210.

49. Chris Burrell, "Papa's Pizza Leaves Leftover Memories," *Vineyard Gazette*, May 10, 2001, https://vineyardgazette.com/news/2001/05/11/papas-pizza-leaves-leftover-memories.

50. *Edible Vineyard*, August 15, 2020.

51. Richard C. Skidmore, "Through the Looking Glass," *Martha's Vineyard*, April 30, 2021, https://mvmagazine.com/news/2021/04/30/through-thelooking-glass.

52. Tina Miller, "When I Opened the Roadhouse," *Edible Vineyard*, October 15, 2021, https://ediblevineyard.com/2021/10/15/when-i-opened-the-roadhouse/.

53. *MV Times*, January 25, 2024.

Chapter 11

54. Vineyard Square Hotel, "Is There a Vineyard on Martha's Vineyard?" https://www.vineyardsquarehotel.com/is-there-a-vineyard-on-marthas-vineyard/.

55. Ibid.

56. *Vineyard Gazette*, May 20, 1966.

57. Doug Cabral, "An Oral History of the Last Real Bar on Martha's Vineyard," *Boston*, July 25, 2019, https://www.bostonmagazine.com/restaurants/2019/06/25/ritz-cafe/.

58. Connie Berry, "Homegrown Hops," *MV Times*, September 16, 2020, https://www.mvtimes.com/2020/09/16/homegrown-hops/.

59. Julia Rappaport, "The Last Grape: Chicama Vineyards Closes Its Cellar," *Vineyard Gazette*, August 11, 2008, https://vineyardgazette.com/news/2008/08/12/farm-and-field.

60. Frank J. Prial, "Family Winery: The Mathiesens' Vineyard Is on Martha's," *New York Times*, October 24, 1974, https://www.nytimes.com/1974/10/24/archives/family-winery-the-mathiesens-vineyard-is-on-marthas-less-time-for.html#after-story-ad-1.

61. Rappaport, "Last Grape."

62. Darlene Cocherell of Madison, Ohio, emailed the *Vineyard Gazette* in 2014.

63. Rappaport, "Last Grape."

64. Ibid.

Chapter 12

65. Miller and Matheson, *Vineyard Harvest*, 237.

Chapter 13

66. Vaughn Barmakian, "Penny Candy Memories of Oak Bluffs," *Vineyard Gazette*, March 8, 2017, https://vineyardgazette.com/news/2017/03/08/penny-candy-melody-oak-bluffs-memories.

67. *Vineyard Gazette*, February 27, 1970.

68. Skip Finley, "Oak Bluffs Town Column: May 17," *Vineyard Gazette*, May 16, 2013, https://vineyardgazette.com/news/2013/05/16/oak-bluffs-town-column-may-17.

69. Chris Baer, "This Was Then: Darling's," *MV Times*, April 27, 2016, https://www.mvtimes.com/2016/04/27/this-was-then-darlings/.

70. Email from Arne Carr, November 4, 2023.

71. Phyllis Meras, "A Fond Adieu to Darling's of Oak Bluffs Where Popcorn Was Pure Island Magic," *Vineyard Gazette*, June 12, 1981, https://vineyardgazette.com/news/1981/06/12/fond-adieu-darlings-oak-bluffs-where-popcorn-was-pure-island-magic.

72. *Vineyard Gazette*, October 6, 2023.

73. Joseph D'Eramo, "Murdick's Fudge Celebrates 40 Years on Martha's Vineyard," Patch, November 15, 2017, https://patch.com/massachusetts/plymouth/murdick-s-fudge-celebrates-40-years-marthas-vineyard.

74. Brian Dowd, "Chilmark Chocolates to Close by the End of the Year," *MV Times*, February 7, 2019, https://www.mvtimes.com/2019/02/07/chilmark-chocolates-close-doors-end-year/.

75. Will Sennott, "Ending an Era, Chilmark Chocolates Closes Its Doors," *Vineyard Gazette*, December 18, 2019, https://vineyardgazette.com/news/2019/12/18/chilmark-chocolates-closes-its-doors-last-time.

76. Gwyn McAllister, "The Flanders Sisters' Salt Rock Chocolates," *Bluedot Living*, August 8, 2022, https://marthasvineyard.bluedotliving.com/2022/08/08/the-flanders-sisters-salt-rock-chocolates.

Chapter 14

77. Thomas Dresser, "Gift of Gleaning Sprouts All Year Long," *Vineyard Gazette*, December 20, 2021, https://vineyardgazette.com/news/2021/12/20/gift-gleaning-sprouts-all-year-long.

78. Lucas Thors, "Local Hero: Rebecca Haag," *Bluedot Living*, September 7, 2023.

Chapter 15

79. Joseph Chase Allen, "President Kennedy Slept in Room L at Ocean View, and This Is How It Happened, Rep. Sylvia Recalls," *Vineyard Gazette*, December 29, 1961, https://vineyardgazette.com/news/1961/12/29/president-kennedy-slept-room-l-ocean-view-and-how-it-happened-rep-sylvia-recalls.

80. "The Sea View House Is Remembered 140 Years Later," *Martha's Vineyard Times*, July 18, 2012, https://www.mvtimes.com/2012/07/18/sea-view-house-remembered-140-years-later-11486/.

81. *Vineyard Gazette*, April 29, 1938.

82. *Vineyard Gazette*, June 18, 1954.

83. *Vineyard Gazette*, February 19, 1956.

84. Ethan Genter, "Plan to Rebuild Ocean View Restaurant Will Include Apartments," *Vineyard Gazette*, May 14, 2023, https://vineyardgazette.com/news/2023/05/14/plan-rebuild-ocean-view-restaurant-will-include-apartments.

85. *Vineyard Gazette*, June 30, 1931.

86. Geoff Currier, "Where There's a Will, There's a Way," *MV Times*, December 9, 2020, https://www.mvtimes.com/2020/12/09/theres-will-theres-way/.

87. *Martha's Vineyard Times*, December 26, 2012.

88. Records of the Worcester Car Lunch Company, housed at the Worcester Historical Museum, 1998.

89. *Vineyard Gazette*, October 11, 1963.

90. Ibid.

91. *Vineyard Style*, 2013.

92. Lisa C. Belcastro, "The Art Cliff Celebrates Seventy Delicious Years," *Vineyard Style*, Winter 2013, https://vineyardstyle.com/marthas-vineyard-archive.php/140/The-Art-Cliff-Celebrates-Seventy-Delicious-Years.

93. Susie Middleton, "Gina Stanley's Art Cliff Diner: A Seventeen-Year Lover Affair," *Cook the Vineyard*, August 3, 2017, https://mvmagazine.com/news/2019/06/06/gina-stanleys-art-cliff-diner-seventeen-year-love-affair.

94. Connie Berry, "ArtCliff Diner: One Cliff I'd Definitely Go Over," *MV Times*, November 28, 2017, https://www.mvtimes.com/2017/11/28/artcliff-diner-one-cliff-id-definitely-go/.

95. Laura Holmes Haddad, "The Hunt for Cider Donuts: Where to Find Them On-Island," *Cook the Vineyard*, October 30, 2023, https://mvmagazine.com/news/2023/10/30/hunt-cider-donuts-where-find-them-island.

96. Sam Houghton, "Iconic Aquinnah Restaurant Sold to Native Land Group," *MV Times*, August 18, 2023, https://www.mvtimes.com/2023/08/18/iconic-aquinnah-restaurant-sold-native-land-group/.

97. Email from Virginia Yorke to the *Vineyard Gazette*, June 5, 2023.

98. Eunki Seonwoo, "Beloved Aquinnah Restaurant May Reopen," *MV Times*, February 22, 2024.

99. *Edible Vineyard*, August 12, 2021.

100. Brooke Kushwaha, "The Square Rigger Comes Under New Ownership," *Vineyard Gazette*, December 20, 2022, https://vineyardgazette.com/news/2022/12/20/square-rigger-comes-under-new-ownership.

101. Nicole Jackson, "'New' to Town," *MV Times*, March 22, 2023, https://www.mvtimes.com/2023/03/22/new-to-town/.

102. Riis Williams, "A Second Chapter for Linda Jean's Restaurant," *Vineyard Gazette*, February 14, 2023, https://vineyardgazette.com/news/2023/02/14/second-chapter-linda-jeans-restaurant.

103. Brian Dowd, "Dock Street Is an Edgartown Favorite," *MV Times*, January 2, 2019, https://www.mvtimes.com/2019/01/02/an-edgartown-favorite/

104. Lucas Thors, "In the Woodlands," *MV Times*, March 20, 2019, https://www.mvtimes.com/2019/03/20/in-the-woodlands/

105. Chris Burrell, "Islanders Flock to the In Place: Woodland Grill," *Vineyard Gazette*, December 12, 2002, https://vineyardgazette.com/news/2002/12/13/islanders-flock-place-woodland-grill.

SELECTED BIBLIOGRAPHY

Publications

Diamond, Jared. *Guns, Grains, and Steel*. New York: Random House, 2013.

Dresser, Thomas. *African Americans of Martha's Vineyard*. Charleston, SC: The History Press, 2010.

———. *Martha's Vineyard in the American Revolution*. Charleston, SC: The History Press, 2021.

———. *The Rise of Tourism on Martha's Vineyard*. Charleston, SC: The History Press, 2020.

———. *A Travel History of Martha's Vineyard*. Charleston, SC: The History Press, 2019.

Dunlop, Tom. *Morning Glory Farm*. Edgartown, MA: Vineyard Stories, 2009.

Hall, Joseph, and Ellen Sullivan. *The Black Dog Summer on the Vineyard Cookbook*. Boston: Little, Brown and Company, 2000.

Harris, Jessica. *High on the Hog*. New York: Bloomsbury Publishing, 2012.

———. *Martha's Vineyard Table*. New York: Chronicle Books, 2021.

———. *My Soul Looks Back*. New York: Scribner, 2017.

Holtham, Will. *The Home Port Cookbook*. Guilford, CT: Lyons Press, 2011.

King, Louise Tate, and Jean Stewart Wexler. *The Martha's Vineyard Cook Book*. New York: Harper & Row, 1971.

Lee, Linsey. *Edible Wild Plants of Martha's Vineyard*. Vineyard Haven, MA: Tashmoo Press, 1975.

————. *Vineyard Voices*. Edgartown, MA: Martha's Vineyard Historical Society, 1998.

Miller, Tina, and Christie Matheson. *Vineyard Harvest: A Year of Good Food on Martha's Vineyard*. New York: Bantam Dell Pub Group, 2005.

Sacred Heart Parish Cookbook. Waseca, MN: Walter's Publishing Company, 1980.

Schofield, Jay. *Truly Blessed: The Life Story of Ralph Brown*. Vineyard Haven, MA: Vineyard Memoirs, 2001.

Sherman, Ethel. *The West Tisbury Farmers Market*. Oak Bluffs, MA: DaRosas Corporation, MV Printing Company, 2003.

Periodicals

Bluedot Living
Edible Vineyard
Martha's Vineyard Magazine
Martha's Vineyard Times
New York Times
Vineyard Gazette
Vineyard Style

INDEX

A

Alley, Kerry 49, 50

C

caldo verde (kale soup) 46, 50
Carr, Arne 133
Christie, Lisa and Winston 171
Coutinho, Ginny 46, 47

E

Esposito, Charlie 168, 169

F

foraging 17, 18, 19, 75, 77, 175

G

Giordano, Buster 150, 151
gleaning 78, 79, 80, 81, 140

H

hardtack 37, 38
Harris, Dr. Jessica 19, 20, 53, 58

I

Island Grown Initiative 59, 60, 78,
    79, 80, 81, 140

L

lobster 37, 40, 41

O

Orange Peel Bakery 19, 20, 21, 29

P

potted meats 31

R

Rebello, Todd 94

S

Shearer Cottage 55
soul food 54
Stam, Peter 112
Stanley, Gina 160
swordfish 38, 39

T

taverns 27, 28, 29, 30
Thomas, Chef Deon 58, 59

V

Vanderhoop, Juli 18, 19, 20, 21,
    22, 75

W

whales 37, 38, 45

AUTHORS' NOTES

Growing up in central Massachusetts in the 1950s, neither of our families had occasion to dine out very often. Money was tight. Restaurants were few.

In both the Dresser and Cournoyer households, the mother ran the kitchen, bought the groceries, and prepared the meal. Joyce's father had a vegetable garden. Tom's mother had a garden. No one brought an iPhone to the dinner table, nor was there a TV in the dining room.

Joyce and Tom knew each other in junior high and through high school. We each went our own way through college, marriage, and parenting. Joyce taught school on Martha's Vineyard; Tom taught at Fort Devens, then segued into nursing home administration.

We got together at our thirtieth high school reunion in 1995. Joyce casually invited Tom down to the Island for a weekend.

In 2023, we celebrated our twenty-fifth wedding anniversary.

It's been one long lovely weekend.

For more information, visit thomasdresser.com or email us at thomasdresser@gmail.com or dresserjoycec@gmail.com

Tom and Joyce enjoyed the Crop Walk, raising money to feed the hungry on the Vineyard and around the world. Kutter enjoyed the walk as well. *Courtesy of Joyce Dresser.*

BOOKS BY THOMAS DRESSER

Mystery on the Vineyard (2008)
African Americans of Martha's Vineyard (2010)
The Wampanoag Tribe of Martha's Vineyard (2011)
Disaster off Martha's Vineyard (2012)
Women of Martha's Vineyard (2013)
Martha's Vineyard in World War II (2014)
Music on Martha's Vineyard (2014)
Martha's Vineyard: A History (2015)
Hidden History of Martha's Vineyard (2016)
Whaling on Martha's Vineyard (2017)
A Travel History of Martha's Vineyard (2018)
The Rise of Tourism on Martha's Vineyard (2019)
Ghosts of Martha's Vineyard (2020)
Martha's Vineyard in the American Revolution (2021)
Martha's Vineyard in the Roaring Twenties (2022)
Black Homeownership on Martha's Vineyard (2024)
A Culinary History of Martha's Vineyard (2024)

Visit us at
www.historypress.com